Grate 5oz toasted walnuts, soak in m&
Mammy, Plum Pudding
Lo

T0299503

Lettera 22

Home Kitchen

Everyday cooking made
simple and delicious

Home Kitchen

Everyday cooking made
simple and delicious

Design and photography by Dave Brown
Food styling by Lizzie Kamenetzky

Donal Skehan

Hungarian Chocolate Cake ~ serves 8-10. preheat oven to 180C/350F/gas 4

fine dried breadcrumbs for sprinkling
7oz. plain cooking chocolate
4oz butter . 6oz cas.sugar 5 eggs separated
2 oz. self raising flour
3 oz. ground hazelnuts

① Lightly grease Round tin 8" & 4" deep - loose based. Sprinkle in breadcrumbs & rotate to coat sides.

② Place chocolate in a bowl set over a pan of hot water & leave to melt stirring oceas. Remove bowl & leave to cool. Beat butter & sugar together in a large bowl until pale & fluffy. Add egg yolks & melted choc. & beat until smooth. Stir. in flour & g. nuts

③ Whisk the egg whites until stiff. Fold egg whites into cake mixture. Spoon into prepared tin. Bake app. 40 mins until well Risen. When ready leave to cool for 2 mins. Turn out on to Rack & leave to cool completely.

Fillings

9 oz. marscapone cheese
2 tablespn wh. cream.
9oz cooking choc cut into pieces
1 tablespn. Amaretto

Beat the marscapone cheese & cream together until soft. Place the choc. in a bowl & set over hot water to melt. Remove & beat into cheese mixture with the Amaretto.

9 oz. butter
7 oz. icing sugar
1 tablespn Rum
1 Egg + 2 egg yolks
2 teaspn plain flour
3 tablespn inst. coffee dissolved
4½ oz. plain chocolate in pieces
2oz. butter.

Divide the cake into 4 Rounds & fill with alternate fillings

CONTENTS CONTENTS CONTENTS CONTENTS

Introduction: Notes from a home kitchen 11

1. Make Ahead Sundays 29

2. Everyday Dinners 55

3. Weekday Rush 81

4. Slow Weekend Cooking 117

5. Little Food Wins & Flavour Makers 173

6. Dessert Collection 213

Index 250

Acknowledgements 254

INTRODUCTION

People often say that the kitchen is the heart of the home and, while I believe that to be true, my personal journey to finding where home is (never mind the kitchen) has not been straightforward over the last seven years. That being said, our path to finding our forever home has been one I wouldn't change, and ultimately it has given me a better understanding of just what it means to make a home: a place to feel grounded, to provide security for loved ones and, of course, to make memories through the food we cook and share.

My wife Sofie and I left our little cottage in my home town of Howth, near Dublin, in 2015 for the bright lights of Los Angeles. Our cottage had been a special place for us: our first home and the place where we pretended to be grown-ups throughout our twenties. It had served us well as I settled into writing cookbooks and filming TV shows, most of which were produced from the two tiny front rooms. Looking back at the kitchen there, it truly was the heart and soul of the place. None of our friends had a space like it, and so every weekend it became the place we'd all hang out. The Tardis-like cottage came with an old garden that had formerly been a farmyard, complete with troughs I transformed into a sweet little herb garden flanked by a tangle of nasturtiums that would burst into life every summer. When we arrived, the upper level of the garden was a forest of overgrown grasses and brambles that we hacked back to create a vegetable garden. Summer provided us with a bounty of peas, broad beans and salad leaves, and a glut of cabbages. Our landlord gave us a garden shed, which we painted red and white as an homage to Sofie's Swedish roots. Our neighbours got a kick out of shouting over the wall whenever the poorly placed fire alarm would announce to the entire neighbourhood that is was dinnertime.

That cottage was home, and we celebrated so many milestones there: adopting our pup Max (who is still going strong at 11 years old), cooking our first shared Christmas dinner, and celebrating our engagement and our wedding. All these moments were marked with home-cooked meals, bottles of fizz and suppers with friends perched on charity-shop chairs (we'd push the coffee table together with the kitchen table to make enough space for everyone).

In 2012, I started an annual tradition of appearing on *The Today Show* on NBC for Saint Patrick's Day. They needed a token Paddy to cook traditional fare and I was their man. That life-changing experience began the conversation around exploring the world of food TV and other possibilities in the States. On one early trip, my agent had set up 25 separate meetings, all of which I had come out of thinking that I'd aced it and that the jobs would come rolling in. Not a single callback! After a couple of years of meetings back and forth in New York and Los Angeles, with plenty of failed attempts and misfires, I managed to secure a TV show and a contract with the cable channel Food Network. It was a total pinch-me moment – there I was, co-hosting a competition show with Tia Mowry, whom I had grown up watching on Nickelodeon. With job security in the bag, we gave notice to our landlord.

The sunshine, the space and the allure of the palm tree-lined streets meant it was always going to be Los Angeles where we chose to settle while stateside. On one of our last trips to the city before we moved there, we rented bikes on Venice Beach as the sun was setting and cycled to Santa Monica. It was mid-February and we were in T-shirts, fully appreciating the break from Ireland's cold winter months. After a few whirlwind years of filming TV shows and promoting books, it felt like an escape and a little slice of anonymity I didn't know I needed. We spent the first year travelling back and forth and living out of Airbnbs before finding a house in Eagle Rock, away from all the stereotypically glamorous pitfalls the city normally offers new residents. In East LA, between Pasadena and Glendale, we found community and friendship.

We officially moved to the city in early January, arriving late one night, jet-lagged and with our lives in our suitcases. Bar some core pieces of furniture, our new house was bare, so at 11pm we walked to Target and filled two shopping trolleys with bed sheets, towels and other household essentials. We wheeled the trolleys back up the hill and laughed to ourselves at the idea that the neighbours would definitely know the Irish had arrived when they spotted the two of us hoofing carts up the hill.

Our new neighbourhood would regularly see streets being cordoned off for filming. Movies like *Clueless* and *Reservoir Dogs* had been filmed there, and Ben Affleck and Matt Damon had famously written the script for *Good Will Hunting* while living in the area. Parrots and peacocks were to be found in the trees, while coyotes, possums and skunks roamed through the gardens at night. It was wild, weird and wonderful, and a million miles away from everything I had grown up with. I loved it. I wrote three cookbooks in the local coffee shop, Found – a great spot for people-watching.

I was surrounded by artists sketching on iPads, uber-cool parents with sunglasses and strollers, and film industry people. All pretty inspiring for the Irish fella writing recipes in the corner and trying to blend in with an order of espresso with tonic water.

The biggest surprise I got in Los Angeles was the food. Despite rumours to the contrary, there was much more to LA than green juice and kale. I discovered that the city had a lot to offer in terms of tastes and flavours; in fact, the cuisine was complex, much like the make-up of the city's diverse inhabitants. The beating heart of LA's food scene was found on street corners, at food trucks, in strip malls and at pop-ups – far from the 'safe' and ultimately bland hyped-up restaurants designed for the in-crowd to fawn over.

It was the sheer amount of food options that inspired me the most. In our neighbourhood alone, we had Casa Bianca Pizza Pie, an old-school pizza joint with signed photos of Hollywood stars on the wall, while close by, a Tijuana-style taco stand served tacos *al pastor* from a huge spit.

IT WAS THE SHEER
AMOUNT OF FOOD
OPTIONS IN OUR
NEIGHBOURHOOD
THAT INSPIRED
ME THE MOST.

The women who served at the stand only spoke Spanish, but we'd always have great chats in broken Spanish as they cooed over our eldest, Noah, and his shock of blond hair; he would happily put up with it, as they always offered him a tortilla with a little cheese in to keep him happy. I became a regular at Seafood City, the Filipino supermarket in the Eagle Rock plaza. I would often get quizzed by Filipino moms while queuing up at the meat counter; they'd ask why I was shopping there, assuming I had a Filipino wife.

One neighbourhood over, Highland Park, was a perfect example of what gentrification looked like. Spanish food shops sat next to stores decked out in macrame, smelling of palo santo and selling crystal singing bowls for hundreds of dollars. Every Tuesday night, food stalls would pop up, selling everything from vegan tacos to hand-pulled biang biang noodles, which were slapped in front of you before being coated in numbing Sichuan peppercorn-laden oil. We spent many evenings grazing between Chef Nancy Silverton's Triple Beam Pizza, which served up Roman-style pizza by the slice, and Mason's Dumplings, which served incredible pan-fried handmade dumplings.

The San Gabriel valley to the south-east of Eagle Rock is home to one of the largest Asian American populations in the US, and as a result, the food was fantastic. We discovered the most authentic versions of Sichuan cuisine – our favourite place served toothpick lamb and water-boiled beef, which came with a tableside addition of boiling oil. This was poured over the slices of beef and chillies to create a plume of aromatics that would envelop the table. We devoured rich broths served in Vietnamese pho spots like Golden Deli, and proper bánh mì served from unassuming little joints. Hunting them down required plenty of trial and error, and I spent most weekends in LA trying out places I'd found online or that had been suggested by someone I'd met. One of the best tips I got was from a chef friend who used to head to a Thai breakfast restaurant before shopping at the Hollywood Farmers' Market on Sundays. This became our most regular routine: it was the perfect place for sleep-deprived parents, as it began slinging out bowls of congee with softly poached eggs, spring onions, white pepper and little pork meatballs from 6am. With full bellies and buzzing from Chinese-style doughnuts and coffee laced with condensed milk, we'd browse the stalls, which teemed with unusual (to us) items like Pakistani mulberries, hachiya persimmons, purple napa cabbage and rainbow radishes – it was as if all the vegetables I had ever known were now in technicolour. On one visit, I bumped into Alicia Silverstone, and I also spotted famous *LA Times* food writer the late Jonathan Gold in a chance encounter. I will forever regret not thanking him for his many wonderful food recommendations, which I had followed unwaveringly, and had inspired us to explore the city fully while we lived there.

Cooking at home changed for me in LA. Coming from Ireland, a takeaway was a treat: maybe beef and black bean sauce with fried rice and prawn crackers. In LA, eating out was standard; doggy bags of leftovers became the norm, and dinner was rarely eaten at home. When we did cook, we were lucky enough to have a modern kitchen in our rental and the full run of a big American-style oven, hob and hood that is still one of the best pieces of kitchen kit I have used. Our garden was a treasure trove of fruit trees. At its centre was a huge old avocado tree, which had seen better days, and from which we only ever managed to gather an armful of fruit every year, despite its size; the squirrels would devour the rest. To the side of the house there were two lemon trees, which meant we never bought a single lemon in the entire time we lived there. Even when they weren't fully in season, there would always be plenty of fruit on the tree. Out the front stood a glorious fig tree that produced the most spectacular purple fruit, which we ate straight from the tree and turned into jam from early summer right through to autumn.

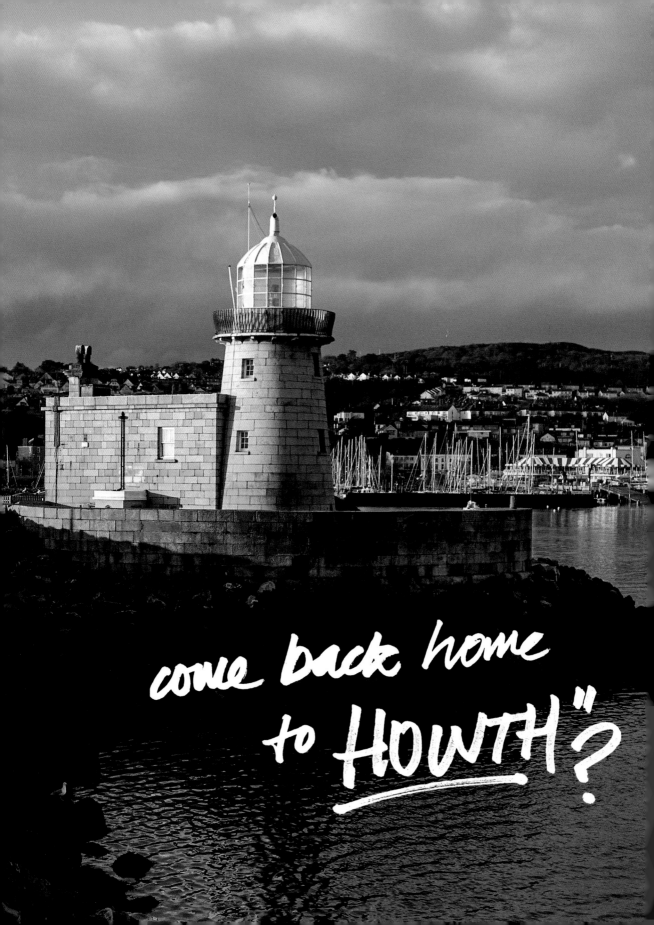

come back home to HOWTH"?

Coming home to Ireland in 2020 after five years of living in Los Angeles was not an easy decision. The seed was planted in the summer of 2018 when we took our eldest, Noah, home for one of his first visits to see family. Being back in the house where I'd grown up with my wife and our six-month-old was a strange feeling. He was sleeping in my childhood bedroom, in the cot I'd slept in as a baby. It had been passed down through our family and a few of my cousins had taken their turns to pull at the bars, gnaw at the wooden slats that held it together, and basically tear it apart. My parents had kept it, perhaps for this precise moment. The result was a true sense of nostalgia, mixed with hilarity over the state of the cot in which our little guy was meant to sleep soundly. But sleep soundly he did – much to our joy, after months of bleary-eyed, new-parent struggles. My parents offered to keep an ear out for him while Sofie and I took a walk down to the pier in Howth. We strolled through the village and caught the most beautiful sunset together, sitting by the lighthouse at the end of the East Pier. For the first time, we both felt a sense of security we hadn't been aware we'd been missing while living so far away. I had often described living away from home as being like treading water in the middle of a deep swimming pool; on that trip home, there was suddenly the feeling of having one hand safely on the side, anchoring me. We had loved the adventure of everything that Los Angeles had brought us, but in that moment, we knew what we had ultimately been searching for was home.

My grandad's death at the start of 2020 was the beginning of the end of our time in California. Our second son, Oliver, was born within a couple of weeks of his passing, and it wasn't possible for us to travel home to be with my family and mourn his passing. Instead, I sat and watched the funeral with tears rolling down my face via a live link, 6,000 miles away. In the dark of our bedroom, while a newborn lay peacefully beside me, I watched on as my grandad was laid to rest. On my last couple of trips home, I had seen him go

from the house he had lived in with my grandmother before her death to the nursing home where he was taken care of in his final days. He had got great joy from meeting his only great-grandchild and never failed to repeat his enduring query and mantra of 'Do you ever think you'll come home to Howth?' I never had a clear answer for him when he asked, but in that moment, so far removed from my entire family at such a significant time, and yet surrounded by my own young family, I knew we were on our way.

We left LA in the flurry of fear as Covid restrictions descended on the world. There was a growing sense of anxiety as our gentle move home turned into a bit of a nightmare. Our plans had to be expedited, and in a matter of weeks we had wrapped up our lives and packed everything off to Ireland in a shipping container. Three cancelled flights, the pup getting stuck in an airport on another continent, and of course the fear of the virus itself made us question ourselves so many times as we ferried our two young children back to Ireland. Noah, who had just turned two, seemed oblivious to it all, but I knew he could sense the tension as we scrambled to arrange everything and find a house back home. The rush and the backdrop of stress and fear was not how we had planned to say goodbye to what we will always look back on as a special chapter in our lives.

We landed in a heap in Sutton House (which we had only seen pictures of online), an old Victorian house that was cold, rickety and filled with ornate, dusty furniture. Our own furniture wasn't due to arrive for another couple of weeks, so we made do with what we had. The kitchen was a nightmare: *Downton Abbey*-style, with a wooden dresser at one end and an old Aga at the other. Along each side of the room were built-in wooden cupboards, while the electric stove with broken knobs burnt everything. I battled daily with drawers that never went in or out smoothly. No matter how we reorganised it, it never worked.

The saving grace of the house was a little secret spot at the end of the garden. In the midst of the madness of lockdown, it was somewhere to escape to. My morning routine on sunny days was to make a moka pot of Italian coffee and read a cookbook for a while before the kids would find me.

Word had got out that 'yer man off the telly' had moved into the neighbourhood, and within a couple of days our new next-door neighbour Sandra got a bit ahead of herself with all the excitement, letting herself in the back door to drop in a pack of goodies. We knew we were back home as it was something that would never happen with our neighbours in Los Angeles! The surprise of seeing a stranger in our kitchen was clearly visible on our shocked faces, and she shrieked 'SORRY!' before running back next door! It was all fairly hilarious and well-intentioned, and a solid reminder of the familiarity and warmth Irish people naturally show. After that, we would meet regularly to have conversations through the bushes at the front door, filling each other in on our – at the time – Covid-restricted lives.

With little else to do but focus on what we were going to eat throughout the day, I settled into cooking, despite the nightmare kitchen. I decided to lean in to the things that make eating in Ireland truly special: seasonal vegetables, stonkingly good cheese, fine meat and the freshest seafood. Our house was near a really great butcher and a little further along on the West Pier, was Howth's selection of fishmongers. We indulged ourselves with little feasts for two. The live lobster we bought, which escaped from the bottom of the stroller to skitter across the Victorian tiles of the kitchen, to the squeals of the boys and Sofie, was devoured with a negroni in the back garden. Côte de boeuf was barbecued outside in the late summer and shared on a picnic blanket with homemade aioli. Oliver spread veggie purées across his highchair, while Noah swapped his Californian favourites of

Thai *Jok* rice porridge and *boba* Fridays for lamb chops with potatoes and mussels with crusty bread.

We've been back in Ireland almost three years now, and of course it hasn't been the easiest of transitions; we've since moved two more times while we search for the elusive 'forever home'. I'm still dreaming of my perfect kitchen, but in the process we have found rhythm and routines for our family that are reflected in the way we cook and eat. Despite the uncertainty and many highs and lows of the past few years, we have found solace and comfort in the daily routines and the family tradition of eating together.

I have in the past felt somewhat embarrassed explaining why we have not yet got a secure space where our children can grow up, but I know the path we have taken has been part of shaping who we are as a family. It has provided us with a sense of resilience and a constant reminder to seek out adventure and exploration. Ultimately, we know ourselves that bit more as a result of all our moving, and are now more focused on fighting that bit harder for the things we want. As I sat down to write this in January, we had been holding our breath as we entered the final stages of securing a little house by the sea. It had captured our hearts and, despite its tiny size, I saw its full potential as a home for our family. I dreamed of growing a vegetable garden there, sharing weekends with friends and watching our boys grow up. In a vomit-inducing battle against a fellow bidder, when all was almost lost, I wrote to the seller, partly in desperation and partly in the hope that perhaps our complicated story of returning home might sway our case. Thankfully it worked, and earlier this year we got the keys to our first home, a moment certainly not lost on us after the uncertainty of so many moves. Finally, home.

I recently sat down with the collection of handwritten recipe notebooks my granny kept while raising a

WE BOTH FELT FOR THE FIRST
TIME A SENSE OF SECURITY
WE HADN'T FULLY BEEN AWARE
WE HAD BEEN MISSING LIVING
SO FAR AWAY.

family of seven throughout the 1960s and 70s. They are filled with notes to herself on how to recreate her most treasured meals, little sentences about Sunday dinners from a time long forgotten, and scribbles reminding herself to clean a coffee pot or stoke the Raeburn stove to keep it at an even temperature. Each page is a reminder of the importance food plays in the intricate ins and outs of life. It's a perfect example of the legacy we leave behind for loved ones and generations to come, and the deep influence that the simple act of cooking a meal can leave on those we spend time with.

My aim with this book – as is the case with all the recipes I write – is that it becomes part of your everyday life, too. I hope that my recipes for birthday cakes are revisited every year until the pages grow splattered with batter, or that the Amatriciana Meatballs leave an indelible red-sauce mark on the pages as you prepare them for a Friday night to celebrate the end of the week. Maybe you're just starting out in the kitchen, and you hope to learn how to bake using the recipe for cookies, or perhaps the Fancy Meringue Swish will become your party piece for Sunday dinners.

I'd love the recipes here to serve you as they do our family, with inspiration for just about everything life throws your way. Our week often begins on a Sunday with make-ahead meals that see us through the week, so in the Make-Ahead Sundays chapter, you will find recipes that can be made in advance and will hold up well in fridge or freezer to take the pressure off weeknight mealtimes. Slow-Cooker Beef Ragu, with its deliciously tender meat shredded into a rich sauce, will sit happily, awaiting its moment of glory when stirred through freshly cooked pappardelle; One-Pot Moroccan-Style Meatballs will only improve in flavour as the spices enrich the sauce during an overnight stay in the fridge. With a little advance preparation, the recipes in this chapter will lead to more harmonious meal times.

Staple weeknight dinners that you can rely on – ones that should be an important part of any home cook's arsenal – can be found in the Everyday Dinners chapter. Simple dishes like the Speedy Parmigiana Pasta, Bavette Steak with Banchan and Sticky Caramel Salmon Feast provide inspiration and a base of great meals to choose from when you have to feed a hungry crew.

Cooking on a weeknight is a test of one's fortitude, a battle against the clock and a struggle to maintain one's sanity. But, as with all great battles, the rewards are worth the effort. To be able to put a hot, nourishing meal on the table after a long day of work is a victory that cannot be overstated. It's a testament to our resilience, our resourcefulness, and our ability to find joy in the most ordinary of tasks. So, sharpen your knives, turn up the heat, and let's get to work with the Weekday Rush chapter. Because, when it comes to cooking on a weeknight, the only way out is through. Arm yourself with recipes like Vodka Penne Sausage Ragu, Gnocchi al Limone and Pot Sticker Bowls and you'll find the way.

Standing in my kitchen on a lazy Saturday morning, taking my first sip of espresso, the weekend is full of possibility. No school runs, the pressure is off, and there's something special about taking the time to dream up a meal that will cook for hours, filling the house with fragrant scents and anticipation. The gentle bubbling of the pot on the stove is like a soothing symphony, reminding me to slow down and embrace the moment. The beauty of slow weekend cooking is that it's not just about the end result, but the process, too: the gentle stirring, the careful seasoning, the occasional taste test. It's a reminder that – sometimes – the best things in life take time. Away from the time constraints of weeknight cooking, there's time to tackle Citrusy Harissa Barbecued Lamb Shoulder with Charred Greens, served with cumin salt (a nod to a recent trip to Marrakech), or the Reverse-Seared Côte de Boeuf, with Aioli and Chipped Potatoes, accompanied by a glass of red wine. Family favourites like the Focaccia-Style Pizza will keep the kids happy, while Slow-Roasted Pork Shoulder with Honey & Apple Vinegar Sauce makes a perfect Sunday feast to share with friends and family. The recipes in Slow Weekend Cooking are all about taking some time to slow down, savour the flavours, and enjoy the company of those you love.

I'd love to tell you that all my cooking is well thought through and planned out, but of course it's not. Even with the best intentions I still regularly find myself staring deep into the kitchen cupboard wondering what the hell I'm going to cook. Sometimes, I get my most rewarding results in the kitchen from the little victories,

the small but mighty flavour-makers that sit awaiting deployment to transform your dish. In the Food Wins and Flavour-Makers chapter, kitchen-cupboard heroes like peanut butter, gochujang, soy sauce, chilli oil and jars of spices are celebrated, and you'll find plenty of inspiration and recipes. Think Instant Ramen Upgrade ideas, Fennel & Orange Rubbed Pork Chops and Bang Bang Chicken Salad with its lip-numbing Sichuan peppercorn dressing.

In my mind, no meal or feast is complete without dessert: it's the final act of any great meal, the crescendo that leaves a lasting impression. And when it's a homemade dessert, it's all the more special. It doesn't have to be over the top; often the best reaction is from a recipe you have used time and again, one you know the ins and outs of and one your family and friends will look forward to. Whether it's a trusty chocolate cake wheeled out for birthdays, a fruit galette with buttery homemade pastry or torched boozy bananas over vanilla ice cream, dessert should be uncomplicated and strike a chord of nostalgia. Food so often sparks happy memories and the connections that come with a well-loved recipe; with dessert, that connection is all the sweeter.

I do hope these recipes find a place in your home kitchen and become part of the fabric of your family life, as they have done mine.

DONAL x

Howth, Dublin, Ireland, January 2023

INTRODUCTION

Make-Ahead Sundays

1. Back-to-School Slow Cooker Chicken Stew
2. Chicken & Ginger Rice Soup (Jok)
3. Little Kid/Big Kid Pastina Soup
4. Noah's Chicken Noodle Soup
5. Leftover Roast Chicken Pasta
6. Oven-Roasted Shawarma Chicken & Vegetables
7. Slow-Cooker Butter Chicken
8. Sticky Pork Belly StripsSupper
9. Slow-Cooker Mongolian-Style Beef with Sweet Potatoes
10. Sticky Honey & Five Spice Slow-Cooker Chicken
11. Slow-Cooker Beef Ragu
12. One-Pot Moroccan-Style Meatballs

Serves 4–6

Prep time: 20 minutes

Cook time: 6 hours

Back-to-School Slow-Cooker Chicken Stew

A rich chicken stew that tastes just like a Sunday roast. Chicken thighs are simmered until falling off the bone and the cooking liquor is reduced until thick and gravy-like, all before little cloud-like chive and cheddar dumplings are popped on top to steam and soak up the sauce. This is the type of dish made for those days when the weather starts to turn and you need a bowl of something comforting.

8 chicken thighs (bone in and skin on)

2 tbsp olive oil

30g (1oz) salted butter

1 large onion, thinly sliced

3 celery sticks, chopped

3 large carrots, chopped

2 garlic cloves, grated

3–4 sprigs of thyme

2 tbsp plain (all-purpose) flour

400ml (1¾ cups) chicken stock

Sea salt and freshly ground black pepper

For the dumplings

60g (2¼oz) cold salted butter

150g (generous 1 cup) self-raising flour

Good pinch of salt

1 tbsp snipped chives

100ml (scant ½ cup) buttermilk (or use milk or natural yoghurt)

50g (2oz) grated Cheddar

1. Season the chicken all over with salt and pepper. Heat the oil in a frying pan (skillet) on a medium heat or using the sauté function on your slow cooker. Add the chicken and brown all over, then set aside. Add the butter to the pan and allow to melt, then add the onion, celery and carrots and sweat slowly for 5 minutes. Add the garlic and thyme.

2. Stir in the plain flour, then add the stock and bubble for a minute or two before pouring this over the chicken in the slow cooker. Season well.

3. Cook on low for 5 hours. (Alternatively, you can cook this in a casserole dish, simmering over a low heat for 1½ hours, or in an oven preheated to 160°C/140°C fan/320°F/gas mark 3, again for 1½ hours.)

4. Now make the dumplings. In a bowl, rub the butter and flour together with your fingers until the mixture resembles breadcrumbs then add the salt, chives, buttermilk and cheese, and combine to form a soft dough.

5. Increase the temperature of your slow cooker to high.

6. Roll the dough into walnut-sized pieces and dot all over the surface of the stew. Cover with the lid and cook on high for a further hour before serving.

MAKE-AHEAD SUNDAYS

Serves 4   DF

Prep time: 10 minutes

Cook time: 40 minutes

Chicken & Ginger Rice Soup (*Jok*)

In the early stages of parenthood, breakfast out for us sleep-deprived parents was the ultimate treat. Our weekend routine often involved a trip to Siam Sunset in Thai Town, LA. With its faded blue awning and crumbling facade, it's an unassuming Thai restaurant that you would most likely walk past. Inside was a different story: bustling and busy, it began serving bowls of rice porridge and soup from 6am. Sofie and I would slowly come to life over a Formica table piled with condiments like fish sauce and pickled green chillies, drinking iced coffee with condensed milk. Big bowls of simple rice porridge or soup were slurped while surrounded by the chatter of families speaking Thai to each other, as Noah slept in a car seat on the floor. While my homemade version won't be the same, making it takes me right back to those days.

1 litre (4 cups) chicken bone broth or good fresh chicken stock, plus 200ml (generous ¾ cup) water

4 chicken thighs (bone in and skin on)

3cm (1¼in) piece of fresh ginger, peeled and sliced into matchsticks

1 bunch of spring onions (scallions)

2 kaffir lime leaves

1 lemongrass stalk, bashed

1 tbsp fish sauce

200g (7oz) jasmine rice

4 baby pak choi, halved or quartered

1 red chilli, thinly sliced

3 tbsp soy sauce

3 tbsp rice vinegar

½ cucumber, diced

40g (1½oz) shop-bought crispy onions

30g (1oz) bunch of coriander (cilantro) leaves

1. Put the broth, water and chicken thighs into a large saucepan and add the ginger. Slice half the spring onions into 3cm (1¼in) pieces and add to the pan, along with the lime leaves, lemongrass and fish sauce.

2. Bring to the boil, then reduce the heat and simmer gently for 20 minutes until the chicken is tender and cooked. Remove the chicken from the pan with a slotted spoon and set aside.

3. Add the rice to the soup and cook for at least 20 minutes or up to an hour, until very tender and the liquid has been mostly absorbed. The longer you cook it, the thicker it will get; you can always add more stock if you want to loosen it. If you're making this ahead, you can reheat after this stage and continue following the cooking steps.

4. Shred the meat from the chicken thighs (discarding the skin) and stir into the soup with the baby pak choi.

5. Thinly slice the rest of the spring onions. In a small bowl, combine the chilli with the soy sauce and vinegar.

6. Ladle the soup into four bowls, making sure the rice and chicken are evenly distributed. Spoon over the soy and chilli mixture, then scatter with the sliced spring onions, diced cucumber, crispy onions and coriander leaves.

Serves 4

Prep time: 10 minutes

Cook time: 35 minutes

Tip:

SERVE THIS AS SOON AS THE PASTA IS COOKED
AS OTHERWISE THE PASTA WILL CONTINUE
ABSORBING THE LIQUID.

Little Kid/ Big Kid Pastina Soup

This recipe for an after-school soup is one that I am quite happy to join in eating with our two boys. For younger eaters, soup can be a challenge, which is why this one – thick with finely chopped vegetables and tender pasta – is an easier sell. It's a simple soup, but there are many ways to make it feel fancy. A drizzle of your best-quality extra virgin olive oil, basil leaves stirred through just before serving, and a mountain of superfine grated Parmesan – each or all of these will take this soup to another level. Save your Parmesan rinds and pop them into soups like this as they blip away on the stove to add richness and flavour.

2 tbsp olive oil

1 small onion, finely chopped

2 garlic cloves, crushed

1 carrot, finely chopped

1 courgette (zucchini), finely chopped

Pinch of chilli flakes

1 x 400g (14oz) tin cherry tomatoes

2 tsp red wine vinegar

1 litre (4 cups) fresh chicken stock

150g (5oz) pastina (stelline, orzo, conchigliette)

Sea salt and freshly ground black pepper

For the basil oil

50g (2oz) basil leaves, plus a few extra to serve

5ml (⅓ cup) extra virgin olive oil, plus a drizzle more to serve

To serve

4 slices of sourdough

1 garlic clove, halved

Parmesan cheese shavings

1. First, make the basil oil. Bring a saucepan of water to the boil, then blanch the basil leaves for a few seconds before transferring to a bowl of iced water. Gently squeeze out the water, then whizz in a small food processor with the extra virgin olive oil. Leave to stand for 10 minutes before straining the oil through a fine sieve.

2. To make the soup, heat the oil in a sauté pan (skillet) over a low heat and gently fry the onion, garlic, carrot and courgette for 10–15 minutes until softened. Add the chilli flakes and cherry tomatoes, crushing the tomatoes with the back of your spoon, then add the vinegar and simmer for 10 minutes.

3. Add the stock and season well. Bring to the boil and simmer for a couple of minutes, then add the pasta and cook for 8 minutes until the pasta is just cooked. If you're making this ahead, wait to add the pasta until you're ready to eat.

4. While the soup is simmering, toast the sourdough and rub with the cut garlic clove, then drizzle with a little extra virgin olive oil.

5. Serve the pasta soup with the garlic toast and a drizzle of the basil oil, some basil leaves and shavings of Parmesan.

MAKE-AHEAD SUNDAYS

Noah's Chicken Noodle Soup

Our two boys have always been great eaters – for the most part. Up until the age of about three or four, they would try anything I put in front of them, so I was thrown when suddenly the way something was cut or the particular temperature or colour began to cause uproar at the dinner table (I'm hoping it's a phase, as I know they both love their food). This is why when I do come across a dish that gets the full family seal of approval, I lean heavily into it. We always joked that growing up we could never tell my mom we liked something, as then we'd get it every day the following week, but now I understand. This chicken noodle soup is ideal for winter days, drippy noses and for keeping the peace come suppertime. If you are stuck for time, which I often am, this can be made rather easily in a pressure cooker in about half the time.

1 small free-range chicken

500ml (2 cups) fresh chicken stock

1 bay leaf

1 onion, halved

2 carrots, 1 cut into large pieces, 1 finely diced

2 celery sticks, 1 cut into pieces, 1 finely diced

10 black peppercorns

Handful of parsley stalks

200g (7oz) angel hair pasta (capellini), broken

Good squeeze of lemon juice

Sea salt

1. Put the chicken into a deep saucepan with the stock and top up with enough cold water to just cover the chicken. Add the aromatices – the bay leaf, onion, large carrot and celery pieces, peppercorns and parsley stalks.

2. Bring to the boil, then reduce to a simmer and poach gently for 1 hour until the chicken is tender. Remove the chicken from the pan and set aside.

3. Scoop the aromatics out of the stock with a slotted spoon, then bring back to the boil and simmer until the stock has reduced by a third.

4. Strip the meat from the bones of the chicken, discarding the skin, then shred the meat and return it to the stock, along with the finely chopped carrot and celery and the pasta. Cook for 3 minutes until the pasta is tender, then season with salt to taste. Serve with a good squeeze of lemon juice. If you're making this ahead, don't add the pasta until you're ready to eat.

Serves 4

Prep time: 10 minutes

Cook time: 15 minutes

Leftover Roast Chicken Pasta

My childhood revolved around the Sunday roast. It's probably the best example of the food legacy my grandmother handed down to my mom, and now to me. For a lot of families it's still a lovely anchoring point: whatever the week may throw at you, it's that one day you may have time to really cook in peace without the usual pressures of your Monday to Friday. I also like how a roast chicken can inform the start of your week by using the carcass to make stock or soup, or using the shredded meat in a mayo and lettuce sambo to chase away any Monday gloom, or – indeed – in this rather comforting pasta dish. If you have any leftover gravy from your roast you can add it to the sauce for extra flavour, while goose fat instead of butter will add an extra layer of flavour to the pasta.

2 tbsp salted butter (or goose fat)

1 banana shallot, finely chopped

2 garlic cloves, crushed

2 sprigs of thyme

2 tbsp plain (all-purpose) flour

400ml (1¾ cups) fresh chicken stock

1 fresh bay leaf

300g (10oz) pappardelle or other thick pasta

50ml (scant ¼ cup) double (heavy) cream (or crème fraîche)

150g (5oz) frozen peas

200g (7oz) baby leaf spinach

250g (9oz) leftover chicken, shredded

2 tbsp snipped chives

Sea salt and freshly ground black pepper

1. Melt the butter or goose fat in a pan over a low heat and gently fry the shallot for 5 minutes, then add the garlic and thyme, and cook for a minute or so more. Add the flour and stir for 1 minute until it is a deep golden brown and smells nutty.

2. Gradually add the stock until you have a thick glossy sauce, then add the bay leaf and season well. Simmer gently for 3–4 minutes.

3. Meanwhile, cook the pasta in a saucepan of boiling salted water for 10–12 minutes. Drain, reserving about 100ml (scant ½ cup) of the cooking water.

4. Add the cream and reserved pasta water to the sauce along with the peas and spinach. Cook until the peas have defrosted and the spinach has wilted, then gently stir in the chicken and cooked pasta. Serve with a scattering of chives.

MAKE-AHEAD SUNDAYS

Serves 6

Prep time: 15 minutes,
plus marinating

Cook time: 50 minutes

Oven-Roasted Shawarma Chicken & Vegetables

I like to think I have assembly-style dinners down to a fine art. Whack the oven on, do a little prep on the chopping board and some tossing in a bowl, and then let a baking tray and the heat do the rest. It's the type of supper that can take care of itself, while I take care of whatever mishaps have taken place with our two whirling dervishes. I'll come back to it to assemble on the dinner table once peace has been restored. This chicken baking tray supper does all that and more – with inspiration and spice from the Middle East, it's a shareable feast that can be dinner table-worthy or simply scoffed in front of the telly on a Saturday night. Everything here will reheat well, if you're making this ahead.

8 chicken thigh fillets, cut into three pieces

1 small pumpkin or squash, sliced into wedges

250g (9oz) new potatoes, halved

3 tbsp olive oil

Sumac, for sprinkling

2 tbsp flat-leaf parsley, finely chopped

100g (3½oz) rocket (arugula) leaves

Sea salt and freshly ground black pepper

Flatbreads, to serve

For the marinade

3 tbsp olive oil

1 tbsp ground cumin

2 tsp ground coriander

5 cardamom pods, cracked open

2 tsp smoked sweet paprika

½ tsp chilli flakes

2 tbsp honey

Finely grated zest and juice of 1 lemon

For the sauce

250ml (1 cup) natural yoghurt

2 tbsp tahini

Squeeze of lemon juice

1. In a large bowl, mix together all the ingredients for the marinade, then add the chicken pieces and leave to marinate for at least 3 hours.

2. Preheat the oven to 200°C/180°C fan/400°F/Gas 6. Arrange the pumpkin and potatoes on a very large baking tray (or two baking trays) and drizzle with the oil.

Add the chicken, season well and pour over any of the marinade left in the bowl. Roast for 30 minutes, then turn and roast for a further 15–20 minutes on the other side until the chicken and veggies are tender and everything is a lovely golden brown.

3. Meanwhile, in a bowl, mix together the ingredients for the sauce and set aside.

4. Once everything is ready, transfer the chicken and vegetables to a large serving platter. Sprinkle with the sumac, parsley and rocket, then serve with warm flatbreads and the tahini yoghurt sauce.

Serves 4–6   GF

Prep time: 20 minutes,
plus marinating

Cook time: 6½ hours

Slow-Cooker Butter Chicken

Tip:

IF YOU DON'T HAVE A SLOW COOKER, YOU CAN MAKE THIS IN A LIDDED CASSEROLE DISH AND COOK IN AN OVEN PREHEATED TO 150°C/130°C FAN/300°F/GAS 2 FOR 2–3 HOURS, OR UNTIL THE CHICKEN IS TENDER AND COOKED ALL THE WAY THROUGH.

My kitchen doesn't have too many gadgets, yet, despite some resistance at first, the slow cooker has become a firm fixture that gets pulled out at least once or twice a week. I will always prefer a meal served in a pretty casserole dish, but often needs must – and I admit there is a smug sense of all-day satisfaction that comes from knowing that the little morning prep you've done means you can get on with your day, confident that dinner is all but served. While this is not a traditional butter chicken recipe, in which charred tandoori chicken is smothered in a rich sauce, it still provides wonderful results. You could barbecue or grill the marinated chicken thighs before adding to the slow cooker if you want to add even more flavour.

8 free-range chicken thighs (bone in), skin removed

120ml (½ cup) double (heavy) cream

Steamed rice, to serve

Handful of coriander (cilantro), to serve

For the marinade

400g (14oz) full-fat natural yoghurt

Juice of ½ lemon

1 tbsp garam masala

1 tsp ground coriander

1 tsp paprika

For the curry sauce

40g (1½oz) salted butter

1 tbsp vegetable oil

1 large onion, finely chopped

2 garlic cloves, chopped

3cm (1¼in) piece of fresh ginger, peeled and grated

1 green chilli, deseeded and chopped

4 cardamom pods, cracked

1 tbsp garam masala

1 tsp fenugreek seeds

1 tsp Kashmiri chilli powder

3 tbsp tomato purée (paste)

100ml (scant ½ cup) chicken stock

Sea salt and freshly ground black pepper

1. Put the chicken into a dish with all the marinade ingredients and leave to marinate for at least an hour or overnight.

2. When you're ready to cook the sauce, heat the butter and oil in a frying pan (skillet) over a low heat, or use the sauté setting on your slow cooker. Gently fry the onion, garlic, ginger and chilli for 5–10 minutes until very soft. Add the spices and cook for another minute until fragrant.

3. Tip into your slow cooker (if using a frying pan) and add the chicken thighs, followed by the tomato purée and stock. Season well and cook on low for 6 hours.

4. Carefully remove the chicken to a warmed dish (it will be very tender and falling apart). The sauce will look a little split at this stage, but don't worry – it will come back together. If you're making this ahead, stop here and restart on step 5.

5. Either using the sauté function on your slow cooker or in a pan over a medium heat, reduce the sauce for 5–6 minutes until nicely thickened, then stir through the double cream. Bubble for a few more minutes until you have a rich, creamy sauce. Return the chicken to the sauce and serve with rice and lots of fresh coriander scattered over the top.

Serves 4   DF

Prep time: 15 minutes

Cook time: 1 hour 20 minutes

Sticky Pork Belly Strips Supper

Although pork belly has well and truly had its moment, I still have a thing for the crispy, fatty meat – it goes so well with so many of my favourite Chinese condiments. Rather than tackling the full belly, I've been using packs of pork belly strips in supermarkets, which are fairly inexpensive and quick to cook. This dish is ideal for make-ahead midweek suppers – all of the elements here can be prepared in advance and reheat well. Roast the meat, prepare the cucumber and prep the vegetables; all will sit happily in the fridge for a day or two, awaiting their moment of glory!

1kg (2lb 4oz) pork belly strips

1 tbsp vegetable oil

½ tsp Chinese five-spice

3cm (1¼in) piece of fresh ginger, peeled and grated

2 garlic cloves, bashed

2 tbsp soy sauce

2 tbsp hoisin sauce

1 tbsp rice vinegar

1 tbsp soft light brown sugar

1 star anise

6 baby pak choi or other Chinese greens, quartered

Steamed rice, to serve

For the smacked cucumber

1 large cucumber

1 garlic clove, grated

1 tsp caster (superfine) sugar

1 tbsp soy sauce

1 tbsp rice vinegar

2 tsp Sichuan chilli oil (or regular chilli oil)

1 tbsp toasted sesame seeds

1. Preheat the oven to 200°C/180°C fan/400°F/Gas 6.

2. Toss the pork belly strips in the oil and five-spice. Transfer to a roasting tray with the ginger and garlic. Mix the soy sauce, hoisin sauce, rice vinegar and sugar together with 5 tablespoons water, and pour this over the pork. Add the star anise, then cover the tray with foil and roast for 1 hour until very tender and

sticky. If it is still a little juicy, you can remove the foil and roast for a further 10–15 minutes, turning every so often.

3. Meanwhile, for the smacked cucumber, bash the cucumber with a rolling pin, then roughly cut into chunks. Toss in a bowl with the rest of the ingredients and set aside.

4. Steam the greens in a saucepan over a medium heat with a small splash of water until tender.

5. Serve the sticky pork belly on a bed of rice with the wilted greens and smacked cucumber.

Serves 6   DF

Prep time: 10 minutes

Cook time: 5-8 hours

Slow-Cooker Mongolian-Style Beef with Sweet Potatoes

I have two make-ahead versions of this – the first is when you plonk all the ingredients into a resealable bag and freeze it so you have the bones of the dish at your fingertips whenever you need it. The second option is to cook it in the slow cooker at the weekend and keep it in the fridge until you are ready to serve at some point during the week – the bonus here is that it will only improve in flavour after a couple of days. Serve with steamed rice, spring onions, sesame seeds and coriander to bring it back to life, with some steamed greens on the side, for a meal the whole family will enjoy.

1.5kg (3lb 5oz) flank or skirt steak, cut into large pieces

4 tbsp cornflour (cornstarch)

4 tbsp groundnut (peanut) oil

3cm (1¼in) piece of fresh ginger, peeled and grated

3 garlic cloves, grated

Good pinch of chilli flakes

175ml (¾ cup) light soy sauce

150ml (5fl oz) hot water

2 tbsp soft light brown sugar

800g (1lb 12oz) sweet potatoes, peeled and cubed into 3cm (1¼in) pieces

Sea salt and freshly ground black pepper

To serve

Steamed rice

6 spring onions (scallions), thinly sliced

1 tbsp sesame seeds, toasted

Small bunch of coriander (cilantro), leaves picked

1. Season the steak pieces well and then dredge in the cornflour.

2. Heat the oil in a large frying pan (skillet) over a medium heat and brown the meat (in batches if necessary) until it is really crusty and golden all over. (Alternatively, use the sauté function on your slow cooker.)

3. Add the ginger, garlic and chilli flakes to the pan and fry for 1 minute, then transfer to the slow cooker (unless already using one), along with the soy sauce, water, sugar and sweet potatoes.

4. Cook on high for 5 hours or low for 7–8 hours until super sticky and tender.

5. Serve with steamed rice and scatter with spring onions, sesame seeds and coriander leaves before tucking in.

Serves 4–6

Prep time: 20 minutes

Cook time: 6 hours

Tip:

IF YOU DON'T HAVE A SLOW COOKER, YOU CAN MAKE THIS IN A LIDDED CASSEROLE DISH AND COOK IN AN OVEN PREHEATED TO 160°C/140°C FAN/320°F/GAS 3 FOR 2 HOURS, OR UNTIL THE CHICKEN IS TENDER AND COOKED ALL THE WAY THROUGH.

Sticky Honey & Five-Spice Slow-Cooker Chicken

Make this chicken on a Sunday night and you have the bones of dinner ready to rock for the week ahead. Sticky and tender chicken is the core element here, and you can choose to serve it however you like; a crisp vegetable slaw, rice, or steamed greens would all be good alongside. Tip for extra stickiness: once the chicken is cooked, preheat the grill to high. Put the chicken on a wire rack lined with foil, brush with a good amount of the sauce and pop under the grill until it starts to get sticky and dark.

8 chicken thighs
(bone in and skin on)

2 tsp Chinese five-spice

2 tbsp olive oil

40g (1½oz) unsalted butter

6 garlic cloves, bashed

80g (3oz) runny honey

2 tbsp soy sauce

2 tbsp cider vinegar

2 tsp cornflour (cornstarch)

100ml (scant ½ cup) chicken stock

1 head of broccoli, cut into florets

Sea salt and freshly ground
black pepper

Steamed basmati rice, to serve

1. Season the chicken thighs and rub with the five-spice. Heat half the oil in a large frying pan (skillet) or using the sauté setting on your slow cooker. Brown the chicken thighs all over for 5–6 minutes. Remove and set aside.

2. Add the rest of the oil and the butter to the pan or slow cooker. Add the garlic and cook gently for 1 minute, then add the honey, soy sauce and vinegar. Bubble for 1 minute, then return the chicken and toss to coat. If you're not already using the slow cooker, transfer everything to the slow cooker now,

then cover with the lid and cook on low for 6 hours.

3. Remove the chicken to a warmed plate. Pour the juices into a saucepan over a medium heat or use the sauté function on your slow cooker.

4. Mix the cornflour with 2 tablespoons of the stock, then add this to the pan, along with the rest of the stock. Bubble until you have a thick, glossy sauce.

5. Steam the broccoli until tender. Serve the chicken, rice and broccoli with the sticky sauce spooned over.

Serves 6–8

Prep time: 30 minutes,

Cook time: 8 hours 10 minutes

Tip:

IF YOU DON'T HAVE A SLOW COOKER YOU CAN MAKE THIS IN A LIDDED CASSEROLE DISH. ADD 250-300ML OF FRESH BEEF STOCK INSTEAD OF A STOCK CUBE AND COOK IN AN OVEN PREHEATED TO 150°C/130°C FAN/300°F/GAS 2 FOR 3-3½ HOURS, OR UNTIL THE BEEF IS VERY TENDER.

Slow-Cooker Beef Ragu

I cooked this beef ragu to celebrate my mom's 60th birthday on a family trip to Ostuni in Puglia, Italy, not long after our son Noah was born. I gathered the ingredients from the morning market and the local butchers, and set to work to make a feast for our family. It was a memorable evening – many bottles of wine were consumed and the night was capped off with a dodgy fireworks display, courtesy of my brother. I had made enough of this beef ragu that we all enjoyed it again the following day with no complaints! Whether you are feeding a crowd or making this ahead of time for a family weekday dinner, it works wonderfully in the slow cooker. Beef shin benefits from a low-and-slow cook time, which transforms the tough cut to meltingly tender meat that can be shredded into the rich tomato sauce.

3 tbsp olive oil

100g (3½oz) diced pancetta

1.5kg (3lb 5oz) beef shin, cut into large pieces

2 tbsp plain (all-purpose) flour, seasoned

1 large onion, thinly sliced

2 celery sticks, chopped

1 carrot, chopped

3 garlic cloves, thinly sliced

200ml (generous ¾ cup) white wine

2 x 400g (14oz) tins plum tomatoes

2 fresh bay leaves

2 sprigs of rosemary

½ beef stock cube, crumbled

100ml (scant ½ cup) whole milk

Sea salt and freshly ground black pepper

For the quick garlic toast

8 slices of sourdough bread

1 fat garlic clove, peeled and halved

2 tbsp extra virgin olive oil

To serve

900g (1lb 2oz) dried egg pappardelle

Parmesan cheese shavings

1. Heat the oil in a frying pan (skillet) over a medium–high heat or use the sauté function on your slow cooker. Add the pancetta and fry until it starts to crisp. Scoop out with a slotted spoon and set aside on a plate.

2. Dust the beef pieces in the seasoned flour and brown in batches, adding a bit more oil if you need it. Add the browned pieces to the pancetta as you go.

3. When all the beef has been browned and set aside, add the onion, celery, carrot and garlic to the pan and fry gently for 5 minutes. Add the wine and bubble until reduced by half.

4. Combine the pancetta, beef and veggies together in the slow cooker, then add the plum tomatoes, bay leaves, rosemary and stock cube. Season well and cook on low for 8 hours.

5. Remove the beef from the sauce and set aside in a warmed dish, then add the milk to the sauce and bubble to reduce by a third, either using the sauté function on the slow cooker or in a pan over a medium heat. Shred the meat and return it to the sauce, then bubble together for a further 10 minutes.

6. Meanwhile, prepare the garlic toast. Toast your sourdough and rub all over with a cut garlic clove,

then slowly drizzle with the extra virgin olive oil and sprinkle with flaky sea salt.

7. When you are nearly ready to serve, cook the pasta in a pan of boiling salted water until al dente, following the instructions on the packet. Drain and serve with dollops of the ragu and lots of Parmesan, with the garlic toast on the side.

MAKE-AHEAD SUNDAYS

Serves 4

Prep time: 30 minutes

Cook time: 5 hours

One-Pot Moroccan-Style Meatballs

There are some recipes that are ideal for making ahead of time and seem to improve in flavour once you plonk them in the fridge for an overnight stay. This is particularly true of a tomato-based meatball stew like this one. The spices have an opportunity to mingle with the lamb, the harissa paste has time to develop the deep hum of heat in the sauce, and you are left with a pot of something truly special. Make these while you have time on a Sunday night, and all you have to do to make a meal of them is serve them at the table with rice or couscous, and maybe some flatbreads.

450g (1lb) minced (ground) lamb

½ red onion, finely chopped

2 garlic cloves, crushed

1 medium free-range egg

2 tsp ras el hanout

30g (2oz) fresh white breadcrumbs

1 tbsp finely chopped flat-leaf parsley

2 tbsp olive oil

Sea salt and freshly ground black pepper

For the sauce

1 tbsp olive oil

½ red onion, finely chopped

2 garlic cloves, finely chopped

1 heaped tbsp harissa paste

Grated zest of 1 lemon

400g (14oz) tin chopped tomatoes

100ml (scant ½ cup) chicken stock

400g tin (14oz) chickpeas, drained and rinsed

To serve

Handful of flat-leaf parsley, chopped

Couscous, steamed

Greek yoghurt

Flatbreads, charred and torn

1. In a large bowl, mix the lamb with the red onion, garlic, egg, ras el hanout, breadcrumbs and parsley. Season well and with wet hands, shape into 20 walnut-sized balls.

2. Heat the 2 tablespoons of oil in a frying pan (skillet) or using the sauté function on the slow cooker and brown the meatballs all over. Transfer to a plate.

3. Now for the sauce. Add the 1 tablespoon of oil to the pan or slow cooker and gently fry the onion for 5 minutes, then add the garlic, harissa and lemon zest, and cook for 1 minute more.

4. Transfer to the slow cooker (if you're not already using it), then add the meatballs. Pour over the chopped tomatoes and stock.

5. Season well and cook on high for 4 hours, then add the chickpeas and cook for a further 30 minutes. If the sauce is too juicy at the end, remove the meatballs and reduce to your liking in a pan or using the sauté function on your slow cooker.

6. Serve the meatballs and sauce scattered with parsley, with steamed couscous, a dollop of yoghurt and flatbreads.

Everyday Dinners

1. Winter Sausage Meatballs with Mustard Cream, Greens & Pasta
2. Soy & Honey Orange Mushroom Stir-Fry
3. Speedy Parmigiana Pasta
4. LA Kale Salad with Crunchy Pecorino Croutons
5. VietnameseTurmeric Fishcake Banh Mi
6. Mushroom Al Pastor Taco Night
7. Caramel Salmon Feast
8. Bavette Steak with Banchan
9. Dinner Table Poke Bowl
10. Teriyaki-Glazed Salmon with Rice & Greens
11. Kitchen Cupboard Bean Stew
12. Brie, Mushroom, Truffle & Crispy Bacon Pasta

Serves 6

Prep time: 15 minutes

Cook time: 25 minutes

Winter Sausage Meatballs with Mustard Cream, Greens & Pasta

The cold Irish winter months require stodgy dishes like this one. Sausage meat quality can vary drastically, so do seek out ones you like for this recipe. If you want to make this for a special occasion, try replacing the white wine with Marsala to give a richer flavour to the sauce.

8 herby sausages

2 tbsp olive oil

Good knob of unsalted butter

1 onion, finely chopped

2 garlic cloves, crushed

1 tbsp plain (all-purpose) flour

100ml (scant ½ cup) white wine

200ml (generous ¾ cup) fresh chicken stock

2 tsp Dijon mustard

100ml (scant ½ cup) soured cream or double (heavy) cream

250g (9oz) mafalda or fusilli

300g (10oz) greens (spinach, kale, sprout tops, savoy cabbage), shredded

Salt and freshly ground black pepper

Grated Parmesan cheese, to serve

1. Squeeze the meat from the sausages and shape with wet hands into 30 small meatballs (having wet hands will stop the sausage meat sticking to your hands). Heat half the oil in a large frying pan (skillet) over a medium–high heat and brown the meatballs all over. Set aside.

2. Add the rest of the oil and the butter to the pan, and fry the onion and garlic for 5 minutes. Add the flour and cook for a minute or two, then pour in the wine and bubble for 2 minutes.

3. Gradually pour in the stock until you have a smooth sauce. Season and return the meatballs to the pan, along with the mustard. Stir and simmer for 5–6 minutes until the meatballs are cooked. Stir in the soured cream or double cream.

4. Meanwhile, cook the pasta in a saucepan of boiling salted water for 10–12 minutes until just tender. Drain, reserving a splash of the cooking water, and add this water to the sauce.

5. Steam the greens for 1–2 minutes until just tender, then add to the meatballs and sauce.

6. Serve the pasta with the meatballs and greens spooned on top, with lots of freshly cracked black pepper and a good grating of Parmesan.

EVERYDAY DINNERS

EVERYDAY DINNERS

Serves 4   V DF

Prep time: 10 minutes

Cook time: 15 minutes

Soy & Honey Orange Mushroom Stir-Fry

Many of the meat-free meals that make their way into our weekly rotation rely on mushrooms. I love the flavour and texture they add to so many dishes, and one of my favourite things to do is pan-fry them hard in a hot pan, using a spatula to press them against the hot metal until they turn crisp at their edges and slightly charred. Finished with a little garlic and butter and piled on to grilled sourdough, they might just be one of life's great pleasures. Most supermarkets have a great selection of fungi nowadays, way beyond the white button mushrooms that were the scourge of my childhood. Seek out king oyster mushrooms for their wonderful texture and taste, and you can simply shred them by hand. They are ideal for this crispy stir-fry, which is the perfect meat-free midweek treat.

300g (10oz) mixed shiitake and king oyster mushrooms

50g (2oz) plain (all-purpose) flour

60g (2¼oz) cornflour (cornstarch)

Bunch of spring onions (scallions), shredded lengthways

200ml (generous ¾ cup) vegetable oil, for frying

2 eggs, beaten

4 baby pak choi, halved

Sea salt and freshly ground black pepper

Rice, steamed, to serve

1 tbsp toasted sesame seeds, to garnish

For the sauce

Finely grated zest and juice of 3 large oranges

3cm (1¼in) piece of fresh ginger, peeled and grated

2 garlic cloves, grated

2 tbsp soy sauce

2 tbsp soft dark brown sugar

4 tsp rice vinegar

1 tbsp sesame oil

2 tsp cornflour (cornstarch)

1. Slice or shred the mushrooms into bite-sized pieces.

2. Mix the flours together, then season well.

3. Put the spring onions into a bowl of iced water to help them crisp up and go all curly.

4. For the sauce, combine all the ingredients in a pan and bubble over a medium heat until it has thickened. Keep warm.

5. Heat 5cm (2in) of oil in a wok or large pan until it is shimmering.

6. Dip the mushrooms in the beaten eggs, then coat all over in the flour mixture. Add to the oil and fry in batches for 2–3 minutes until golden and crisp.

7. Scoop out with a slotted spoon and drain on kitchen paper, then add to the sticky sauce and toss together over a low heat.

8. Steam the pak choi for a couple of minutes until tender.

9. Serve the orange mushrooms on a bed of steamed rice, garnished with the curly spring onions, a scattering of sesame seeds and pak choi.

Speedy Parmigiana Pasta

Tinned tomatoes are one of the kitchen essentials I am never without. I sleep well knowing the pantry has at least two tins at the ready. The quality of the contents can have a vastly different effect on the final outcome of the dish you use them in, so do try and seek out tins of high-quality tomatoes, and preferably whole tomatoes where possible. Tomatoes that are grown and produced in Italy tend to be the best; they are not much more expensive yet have a far superior flavour. Aubergine parmigiana is typically a baked dish, but all the elements used here make a really reliable and substantial speedy pasta supper.

50ml (scant ¼ cup) olive oil

2 aubergines (eggplants), cut into 2cm (¾in) cubes

1 onion, finely chopped

2 fat garlic cloves, crushed

3 sprigs of oregano

2 x 400g (14oz) tins plum tomatoes

250g (9oz) rigatoni or other short pasta

Good handful of basil leaves

125g (4oz) ball mozzarella, shredded

20g (¾oz) grated Parmesan cheese (or vegetarian alternative)

sea salt and freshly ground black pepper

green salad, to serve

1. Heat the olive oil in a large frying pan (skillet) over a medium–high heat. Add the aubergine cubes and cook for 10–12 minutes until very tender and lightly golden. (When they are ready, they will release the oil back into the pan.) Remove from the pan with a slotted spoon and set aside on a plate.

2. Add the onion to the pan and cook for 5 minutes, then add the garlic and oregano and cook for 1 minute more. Add the tinned plum tomatoes and crush with the back of your spoon. Season and simmer for 15 minutes.

3. Meanwhile, cook the pasta in a saucepan of boiling salted water for 8–10 minutes. Drain, reserving 100ml (scant ½ cup) of the cooking water. Add the pasta, reserved water and aubergines to the sauce and cook for 1 minute to combine and warm through.

4. Preheat the grill to high. Fold the basil through the pasta parmigiana and tip it into an ovenproof dish. Top with the mozzarella and Parmesan, and lightly fold the cheese into the top of the pasta. Grill for 4–5 minutes until golden and bubbling. Serve with a green salad.

Serves 2 as a main or 4   V
as a light lunch

Prep time: 15 minutes

Cook time: 10 minutes

LA Kale Salad with Crunchy Pecorino Croutons

Our first Airbnb apartment in Los Angeles was a tiny little bedsit above one of the shops on Abbot Kinney Boulevard in Venice. Across the street was GTA, a takeout version of the perpetually popular Gjelina, a staple of the LA food scene. Bubbly, charred-crust pizza with toppings like fontina, truffled goat's cheese, thyme and guanciale, green olives, Fresno chillies and rosemary… all so good and all on our doorstep to take away. They also served up an inspiring set of salads: cabbage and bagna càuda, beetroot and pistachio dukkah and a version of this salad. It's good enough to eat just as is for dinner, though a slice of pizza wouldn't go amiss…

3 tbsp olive oil, plus extra for drizzling

1 fat garlic clove, bashed

Knob of salted butter

125g (4oz) sourdough bread, torn into small pieces

30g (1oz) Pecorino cheese, grated (or vegetarian alternative), plus extra shavings to serve

200g (7oz) kale, tough stems removed and leaves roughly torn

150g (5oz) radishes, thinly sliced

1 large fennel bulb, very thinly sliced

Sea salt and freshly ground black pepper

For the dressing

1 tbsp apple cider vinegar

Zest of 1 lemon

1 tbsp crème fraîche

1 tsp Dijon mustard

2 tbsp extra virgin olive oil

1. Heat the oil in a frying pan (skillet) over a low heat and add the garlic. Fry for 30 seconds until starting to smell fragrant, then add the butter and allow to melt. Stir in the bread and fry for 3–4 minutes until golden brown. Remove the garlic and season the croutons with the grated Pecorino and some salt and pepper.

2. Meanwhile, drizzle the kale with a little olive oil and massage with your hands for a few minutes until it softens. Tip into a serving bowl and add the sliced radishes and shredded fennel, then toss together.

3. To make the dressing, whisk the apple cider vinegar with the lemon zest and plenty of seasoning, then add the crème fraîche and Dijon mustard. Whisk in the extra virgin olive oil, then pour over the salad and toss together.

4. Serve with the crispy Pecorino croutons scattered over the top with some extra Pecorino cheese shavings.

Serves 4

Prep time: 20 minutes,
plus chilling and pickling

Cook time: 6 minutes

Vietnamese Turmeric Fishcake Bánh Mì

Bánh mì is one of my favourite Vietnamese street foods. It beautifully illustrates the French influence on the cuisine, with a baguette containing wonderfully vibrant Vietnamese ingredients. With pâté slathered inside, along with spicy pickled vegetables like carrot and daikon, along with grilled meats, it's obviously at its best eaten at the side of a road after being bought from a vendor who has been making it for years. However, this homemade version can help channel the bustle of Hanoi without the air miles, and takes things a little further by filling the bread with aromatic golden fishcakes. If you can get your hands on fresh turmeric (which freezes well and can be grated from frozen) you can grate a little into the fish cake mixture instead of using dried; it will give a fresher, more zingy flavour. If you want to skip the sandwich form, assemble the fishcakes in bowls with rice noodles and plenty of herbs, and douse with the nuoc cham dressing.

400g (14oz) firm white fish fillets, cut into pieces

30g (1oz) rice flour

1 tsp ground turmeric

2 garlic cloves, grated

2cm (¾in) piece of fresh ginger, peeled and grated

1 tbsp fish sauce

Handful of coriander (cilantro) stalks, finely chopped

2 tbsp iced water

3 spring onions (scallions), very thinly sliced

2 tbsp finely chopped dill

Vegetable oil, for frying

½ large cucumber, peeled, deseeded and sliced into batons

2 carrots, julienne peeled

For the nuoc cham dressing

3 tbsp rice vinegar

1 tbsp fish sauce

Juice of 1 lime

2 tsp palm sugar or soft light brown sugar

1 garlic clove, grated

1 long red chilli, deseeded and finely chopped

To serve

4 tbsp mayonnaise

1 tbsp sweet chilli sauce

4 small baguettes (French sticks)

Large handful of coriander (cilantro), leaves picked

Large handful of mint, leaves picked

1. Dust the fish in the rice flour and put into a food processor, along with the turmeric, garlic, ginger, fish sauce, coriander stalks and iced water. Pulse to form a paste, then add the spring onions and dill and pulse briefly to combine.

2. With wet hands, shape the mixture into 20 small fishcakes. Chill in the fridge for 20 minutes.

3. Meanwhile, whisk together all the ingredients for the dressing. Pour half of this over the cucumber and carrot in a bowl and set aside to pickle for 20 minutes.

4. Heat a thin layer of oil in a non-stick frying pan (skillet) over a medium–high heat and fry the fishcakes for 2–3 minutes on each side until fragrant and golden. You can do this in batches. Remove from the pan and dip into the remaining dressing.

5. Mix the mayonnaise with the sweet chilli sauce and spread inside the baguettes. Fill the baguettes with the fishcakes, pickled cucumber and carrot and herbs, and serve.

Serves 4–6   V

Prep time: 30 minutes

Cook time: 15 minutes

Tip:

DON'T ATTEMPT TO MAKE THIS WITH ANY OLD MUSHROOMS:
IF YOU CAN, SEEK OUT LION'S MANE, MAITAKE OR HEN-OF-THE-
WOOD, AND, OF COURSE, KING OYSTER MUSHROOMS FOR THEIR
TEXTURE AND FLAVOUR. THE TRICK IS TO FRY THEM HARD,
PRESSING THEM WITH THE BACK OF A SPATULA UNTIL THEY
CHAR AND THE EDGES CRISP. THIS WILL GIVE YOU THE BEST
TEXTURE AND FLAVOUR FOR YOUR TACOS.

Mushroom Al Pastor Taco Night

Taco night was probably one of the best things about living in LA. We were spoilt for choice: our neighbourhood of Eagle Rock and nearby Highland Park had plenty of options, but my favourite was Angel's Tijuana Tacos. The team would rock up outside Target on Eagle Rock Boulevard with pop-up awnings and tables early in the evening, and the smell of meat cooking on a spit would entice a line down the block. A warm tortilla, bright salsa and super-smooth guac, along with sliced smoky meat and a flick of pineapple, made for one of the best tacos I've ever tasted. Here I give my gringo version of a vegetarian take on our favourite *al pastor*.

2 tbsp chipotle paste

2 tbsp tomato purée (paste)

4 garlic cloves, peeled and grated

Juice of 1 large orange

1 tsp ground cumin

2 tbsp cider vinegar

2 tbsp olive oil

1 red onion, thinly sliced

250g (9oz) king oyster
mushrooms, torn

200g (9oz) cremini or small
chestnut mushrooms

Large handful of coriander (cilantro),
finely chopped

8 small corn or flour tortillas

Soured cream, to serve

For the pineapple salsa

1 small pineapple, peeled,
cored and cut into wedges

½ red onion, thinly sliced

1 red chilli, finely chopped

1 tbsp extra virgin olive oil

Juice of 1 lime

Small handful of mint leaves,
finely chopped

Sea salt and freshly ground
black pepper

For the guacamole

2 large avocados, pitted and peeled

1 green chilli, deseeded and roughly
chopped (optional)

1 fat garlic clove, grated

4 spring onions (scallions), white
parts thinly sliced

Juice of 1 lime

2 tbsp extra virgin olive oil

Large handful of coriander (cilantro)
leaves, finely chopped

1. To make the sauce, mix the chipotle paste and tomato purée with the garlic, orange juice, cumin and vinegar, then set aside.

2. Heat 1 tablespoon of the oil in a large frying pan (skillet) over a high heat and fry the onion for 5 minutes until softened and slightly coloured, then remove from the pan. Add the remaining oil; once hot, add the mushrooms and fry until golden brown and slightly charred – use the back of a spatula to press the mushrooms against the base of the pan regularly to achieve the best texture. Add the sauce and fry until sticky and reduced.

3. Meanwhile, for the salsa, heat a griddle (grill) pan over a high heat and sear the pineapple wedges all over. Remove from the pan, leave to cool and then finely chop. Mix with the rest of the salsa ingredients, season to taste and set aside.

4. For the guacamole, mash the avocados roughly, then stir in the rest of the ingredients. Season to taste and set aside.

5. Scatter the mushrooms with the coriander and warm the tortillas in a dry frying pan. Serve the mushrooms in the tortillas with the onions, salsa and guacamole and dollops of soured cream.

Serves 4   DF

Prep time: 15 minutes,
plus marinating

Cook time: 15 minutes

Caramel Salmon Feast

This is a Western take on the Vietnamese dish *cá kho*, which is essentially sticky fish baked in a clay pot. Snakehead fish is typically used, but salmon is a good replacement as it can stand up to the aromatics. Thinly slicing the spring onions lengthways takes a little practice and some skill with a knife; once you have them in super-thin pieces, pop them into iced water and they will magically curl up to make a great garnish.

700g (1lb 8oz) salmon fillet, cut into 1–2 cm (¾–1in) strips

3 tbsp fish sauce

1 tsp black peppercorns, bashed in a pestle and mortar

250g (9oz) basmati rice

70g (2¾oz) soft light brown sugar

3cm (1¼in) piece of fresh ginger, peeled and cut into matchsticks

2 garlic cloves, thinly sliced

1 red chilli, finely chopped

4 spring onions (scallions), finely shredded and put into iced water

For the greens

1 tbsp sesame oil

2 garlic cloves, thinly sliced

2 large courgettes (zucchini), spiralised or cut with a julienne peeler

3 pak choi, halved or quartered

2 tbsp soy sauce

1 tbsp sesame seeds, toasted

1. Put the salmon into a dish with the fish sauce and peppercorns and leave to marinate for 30 minutes.

2. Cook the rice in plenty of salted water for 8 minutes. Drain, then return to the pan and cover to steam-dry and finish cooking.

3. Now to the greens: heat the sesame oil in a frying pan (skillet) and add the garlic, courgettes and pak choi. Cook for 2–3 minutes until tender. Add the soy sauce, toss to combine, then transfer to a serving bowl and scatter with the sesame seeds.

4. Scatter the sugar into the base of a large frying pan. Add 3 tablespoons water and stir to combine. Place over a low heat and let the sugar dissolve, then increase the heat until the mixture starts to bubble. Shake any excess marinade off the salmon strips, then add them to the pan and sear on both sides in the caramel. Add the ginger, garlic, chilli and remaining marinade, along with 2 tablespoons water, and cook for 2–3 minutes until just cooked through and lovely and sticky. If the salmon is cooked before the sauce

has reduced to a sticky glaze, you can remove it to a warmed plate with a spatula and then bubble the sauce for 1 minute more before pouring over the salmon to coat.

5. Serve with bowls of rice, the greens and your shredded spring onion garnish.

EVERYDAY DINNERS

Serves 4–6   DF

Prep time: 20 minutes

Cook time: 20 minutes

Tip:

IF YOU CAN'T GET BAVETTE STEAKS, TRY A THICK-CUT RIBEYE. THE CHILLI CRISP CAN BE KEPT FOR WEEKS AT A TIME AND IS PARTICULARLY DELICIOUS DOLLOPED ON TO FRIED EGGS.

Bavette Steak with *Banchan*

Our eating partners in crime in Los Angeles were a couple we met during childbirth classes in Pasadena. With both our firstborns arriving within days of each other we had plenty to bond over. We shared stories of nappies, weaning and sleep schedule secrets over bowls of pho, dim sum, pizza and plenty of wine. When the kids got a little bigger, wine and dinner dates became our thing; one memorable meal was enjoyed in DJ and Grace's back yard under festoon lights and their avocado tree, where we savoured this meat feast while the kids played in the warm evening heat. *Banchan* are small side dishes served alongside cooked rice in Korea. I like the idea of so many elements being made in advance – or at least somewhat prepped in advance; ultimately the core of this recipe comes down to nailing your steak game.

2 x 300g (10oz) bavette steaks, at room temperature (remove from the fridge an hour before cooking)

Olive oil, for rubbing

For the chilli crisp

175ml (¾ cup) light olive oil

3 shallots, thinly sliced

5 garlic cloves, thinly sliced

2 red chillies, thinly sliced

1cm (½in) piece of fresh ginger, finely chopped

Sichuan peppercorns

Flakey sea salt and freshly ground black pepper

For the spinach

500g (1lb 2oz) spinach

2 tsp gochujang

1 tsp caster sugar

1 garlic clove, crushed

1 tbsp soy sauce

1 tbsp sesame oil

1 tbsp sesame seeds, toasted

For the fried cucumber

400g (14oz) small cucumbers

(or 1 large), deseeded and thinly sliced into half-moons

1 tsp fine sea salt

1 tbsp sesame oil

2 spring onions (scallions), thinly sliced

1 garlic clove, crushed

To serve

Steamed rice

Coriander (cilantro) leaves (optional)

Mint leaves (optional)

Kimchi (optional)

1. Start with the chilli crisp. Heat the oil in a small pan over a medium heat and add the shallots, garlic, chillies, ginger and Sichuan peppercorns. Bring to a steady simmer and cook gently for 10–15 minutes or so, stirring regularly, until the shallots and garlic are crisp and light golden. Drain on kitchen paper, then season with flaky sea salt.

2. For the spinach, bring a saucepan of water to the boil, then submerge the spinach for a few seconds. Drain, then quickly plunge into iced water. Squeeze dry and roughly chop, then mix with the remaining ingredients; set aside to marinate.

3. For the cucumber, sprinkle the half-moons with the salt and leave for 10 minutes, then squeeze out all the moisture. Heat the oil in a frying pan (skillet) over a medium heat. Add the spring onions and garlic and cook for a few minutes, then add the

cucumber and cook for a minute or two before scooping out into a bowl.

4. Season the steaks and rub with a little olive oil. Place a heavy-based frying pan over a high heat and fry the steaks for 3–4 minutes on each side until golden brown and still a bit pink in the middle. Rest for 5–10 minutes before slicing. Serve with all the accompaniments.

Serves 4   DF
Prep time: 25 minutes
Cook time: 10–15 minutes

Dinner Table Poke Bowl

This recipe is far simpler than it may sound. Stick the rice in the rice cooker (or cook as per packet instructions), mix together the umami-laden poke-style fish, and prep the spicy mayo and veggies. It's a supper made for weeknight eating! I like to lay all the elements right on the table and let everyone assemble to their heart's content. Don't get caught up trying to track down sashimi-grade fish; the freshest you can get your hands on from a fishmonger will more than likely do the trick. Same goes for the seaweed; here in Ireland, we have an abundance of great seaweed you can find in dried packets and many of them can be used in the mix here for both texture and flavour.

350g (12oz) sushi rice

2 avocados, cubed

1 cucumber, peeled, deseeded and cubed

4 tbsp pickled ginger, drained

2 tbsp black and white sesame seeds, toasted

Furikake seasoning

For the spicy mayo

100g (3½oz) mayonnaise

1 tbsp sriracha

For the salmon and tuna poke

10g (¼oz) dried wakame seaweed

400g (14oz) salmon, preferably sashimi grade, diced

400g (14oz) tuna, preferably sashimi grade, diced

2 spring onions (scallions), thinly sliced

6 tbsp soy sauce

3 tbsp rice vinegar

2 tbsp sesame oil

1. Cook the sushi rice according to the packet instructions.

2. Put the avocado, cucumber, pickled ginger, sesame seeds and furikake seasoning into small bowls.

3. Mix the mayonnaise with the sriracha and put into a bowl.

4. For the poke, rehydrate the seaweed: put into a bowl of cold water and leave for 15 minutes, then drain and pat dry with kitchen paper.

5. Put the salmon into one bowl and the tuna into another. Add the seaweed to the tuna bowl and the spring onions to the salmon. Divide the soy sauce, vinegar and sesame oil between the two fish bowls and stir.

6. Arrange all the bowls on a table with a big bowl of the cooked sushi rice in the centre and let people help build their own perfect poke bowl.

Serves 4   DF

Prep time: 15 minutes,
plus marinating

Cook time: 15 minutes

Teriyaki-Glazed Salmon with Rice & Greens

Tip:

USE SHOP-BOUGHT TERIYAKI SAUCE IF YOU DON'T WANT TO MAKE YOUR OWN.

Our two children are fairly good eaters but like all kids, they go through phases of total dinnertime meltdown. Who knew a perfectly dippy egg yolk touching fried rice could cause absolute carnage, or that a piece of chicken cut the wrong way would result in your toddler turning into a mini dictator? Assembly dinners, like this one with a few different components are often a good bet. Grains, protein and veggies are all prepared separately and assembled the way you like for the adults and arranged on the plate for the kiddos, giving your tiny tyrant very little to grumble about. If you want, pop the rice in a rice cooker, set it and forget it, and add whatever cooked vegetables you fancy to bring this quick-prep supper to the table (I often microwave broccoli, sugar snap peas or green beans for 4 minutes with a little water for perfectly steamed quick-fix vegetables).

4 x 175g (6oz) salmon fillets

200g (7oz) basmati rice

1 tbsp vegetable oil

2 avocados, sliced

½ cucumber, peeled, deseeded and chopped

6 spring onions (scallions), thinly sliced

Salt

For the teriyaki sauce

75ml (¾ cup) soy sauce

50g (2oz) soft light brown sugar

3 tbsp mirin

1 garlic clove, grated

2 tsp cornflour (cornstarch)

1. Mix together the teriyaki sauce ingredients in a small pan over a medium heat and bubble gently for 5 minutes until thickened. Set aside to cool completely.

2. Once cold, pour the teriyaki over the salmon and leave to marinate for at least an hour (overnight is best).

3. Rinse the rice in cold water until the water runs clear. Tip into a pan and cover with 400ml (1¾ cups) cold salted water. Bring to the boil and simmer for 8 minutes, then turn off the heat and leave, covered, to steam. After 5 minutes, all the water will have been absorbed and the rice will be cooked. Fluff up with a fork.

4. Heat the oil in a frying pan (skillet) over a medium–high heat. Remove the salmon from the marinade and fry for 3–4 minutes on one side until sticky and dark, then flip over, add the reserved marinade and cook for a further 2–3 minutes until just cooked. Transfer to a plate.

5. Divide the rice between four bowls. Top each with a salmon fillet, along with some avocado, cucumber and spring onions, and serve.

Kitchen Cupboard Bean Stew

A brothy bean stew made in a flash, particularly if you have a well-stocked kitchen cupboard. Use any beans you fancy, or make it with a mix of two or three types (chickpeas, butterbeans, cannellini beans and kidney beans all work well). Just be sure to drain and rinse them well – and bear in mind that tinned beans are often quite soft and well cooked, so only add them to the pan towards the end of the cooking time. Use your best-quality olive oil and a really good hunk of Parmesan cheese to bring a dish like this to life. Items that go well in the mix if you have them to hand include basil leaves, pancetta, leftover ham or even the dregs of a jar of passata. Adapt and repeat!

2 tbsp olive oil

1 large onion, thinly sliced

2 garlic cloves, thinly sliced

2 tsp dried oregano

900ml (3¾ cups) vegetable stock

200g (7oz) frozen peas, defrosted

400g (14oz) frozen spinach, defrosted

2 x 400g (14oz) tins butterbeans, drained and rinsed

4 slices of sourdough bread

2 tbsp extra virgin olive oil

40g (1½oz) Parmesan cheese (or vegetarian alternative), shaved

Sea salt and freshly ground black pepper

1. Heat the oil in a large pan and gently fry the onion for 5 minutes until softened. Add the garlic and dried oregano and fry for 1 minute more, then add the vegetable stock. Bring to the boil, then reduce to a simmer and cook for 5 minutes.

2. Season and add the vegetables and beans, and cook gently for a few minutes more until everything is warmed through.

3. Meanwhile, brush the bread with extra virgin olive oil and then fry in a hot frying pan (skillet) until golden and crisp on both sides. Slice into wedges and serve with the bean stew, topped with a good drizzle of extra virgin olive oil, freshly ground black pepper and shaved Parmesan.

Serves 4

Prep time: 15 minutes

Cook time: 15 minutes

Brie, Mushroom, Truffle & Crispy Bacon Pasta

I present to you a bowl of just the type of stodge and starch you need after a long week. If it's one of those days, I highly recommend you reach for this completely non-Italian mash-up that breaks many rules – but all in the name of flavour. Brie is stirred through freshly cooked fresh egg pappardelle, with chunks of salty pancetta and garlic mushrooms. If you want a really smooth sauce, you can briefly blitz it with a stick blender once the cheese has mostly melted. Now, truffle purists look away, but a little drizzle of truffle oil won't go amiss in this dish – in for a penny, in for a pound!

1 tbsp olive oil

125g (4oz) pancetta, diced

30g (1oz) unsalted butter

200g (7oz) chestnut mushrooms, sliced

1 garlic clove, thinly sliced

4 sprigs of thyme, leaves stripped

150g (5oz) ripe Brie, at room temperature, diced

150ml (5fl oz) double (heavy) cream

Few drops of truffle oil

250g (9oz) fresh egg pappardelle

Sea salt and freshly ground black pepper

1. Heat the oil in a frying pan (skillet) over a medium–high heat and fry the pancetta until golden and crisp. Remove with a slotted spoon and set aside. Add the butter to the pan and, once foaming, add the mushrooms, garlic and thyme and cook until the mushrooms are golden brown.

2. Meanwhile, gently melt the Brie and cream together in a large saucepan over a low heat. Add the mushrooms, pancetta and truffle oil.

3. Cook the pasta in a pan of boiling salted water for 5–6 minutes, then remove with tongs and add to the pan of cheesy sauce, still over a low heat. Toss to combine, adding a splash more cooking water to loosen if needed, then serve straight away with plenty of freshly ground black pepper.

Weekday Rush

1. Spaghetti with Super-Creamy Mussels
2. One-Pan Fish & Clams with Creamy Peas & Spina ch
3. Pressure Cooker Rotisserie Chicken Pho .
4. Gochujang Butter Fried Rice
5. Prawn Pil Pil Pasta
6. Pork Medallions with Caramelised Onion & Mustard Sauce
7. Gnocchi Cacio e Pepe with Mushrooms & Sage
8. Vodka Penne Sausage Ragu
9. Gnocchi al Limone with Courgette, Peas & Prawns
10. Green Orecchiette with Lots of Pecorino
11. Joy on York Dan Dan Noodles
12. Mushroom & Tofu Rice Bowl
13. Pot Sticker Bowls
14. Cauliflower Mac 'n' Cheese with Chorizo Crumbs

Serves 6

Prep time: 10 minutes

Cook time: 15 minutes

Spaghetti with Super-Creamy Mussels

A bulging net filled with glossy, dark mussels might not be the first ingredient you think to tackle for a midweek meal, but as they cook in minutes they should not be overlooked. These days, those nets seem to be in far better shape than the bags I used to watch my mom pore over after a visit to the fishmonger when I was young; you had to scrub each mussel free of barnacles and beards before you could even begin cooking them. The joy of mussels is that it takes very little to bring them to life: a simple splash of dry white wine with garlic, cream and lemon will burst the shells open to reveal the plump orange meat. Make sure you use the empty shells as makeshift tongs to eat the others with – our boys love this little trick!

400g (14oz) spaghetti or linguine

2 tbsp extra virgin olive oil

3 garlic cloves, thinly sliced

½ tsp chilli flakes

Finely grated zest of 1 lemon

50g (2oz) finely chopped flat-leaf parsley

Toasted sourdough, to serve

Salt

For the mussels

1 tbsp olive oil

1 banana shallot, finely chopped

1kg (2lb 4oz) mussels, cleaned

150ml (5fl oz) white wine

150ml (5fl oz) double (heavy) cream

1. Cook the pasta in boiling salted water for 12 minutes until just al dente, then drain. While the pasta cooks, heat the oil in a frying pan (skillet) over a low heat and infuse with the garlic, chilli and lemon zest. Once the pasta is cooked and drained, toss in the pan with the infused oil and scatter over the parsley.

2. Meanwhile, prepare the mussels: heat the oil in a large saucepan with a lid over a medium heat and gently fry the shallot for 5 minutes until tender. Increase the heat to high,

then add the mussels and wine, and immediately cover with a lid. Cook for 3–4 minutes, shaking every so often, until all the mussels are opened (discard any that remain closed).

3. Using a slotted spoon, scoop out the mussels on to a warmed serving dish. Pour the cream into the pan and bubble the sauce for 1 minute, then pour over the mussels.

4. Serve the pasta with the mussels and creamy sauce spooned over the top.

WEEKDAY RUSH

Serves 4

Prep time: 10 minutes

Cook time: 15 minutes

One-Pan Fish & Clams with Creamy Peas & Spinach

This simple and impressive fish recipe is one to have in your regular rotation. It's elegant enough to serve for a meal with friends but equally speedy enough to serve as a midweek supper. As an island nation, we have a fabulous selection of fresh fish in Ireland, and I try to cook with it as often as I can. As a treat, seek out tiny orange orbs of trout roe, which can be bought in jars and kept in the fridge: Goatsbridge Trout Farm in County Kilkenny is our favourite, and it's delicious with fish dishes just like this.

1 tbsp olive oil

4 x 200g (7oz) firm white fish fillets (such as cod, hake or turbot)

500g (1lb 2oz) fresh clams

150ml (5fl oz) white wine

150g (5oz) frozen peas, defrosted

250g (9oz) baby spinach

75ml (⅓ cup) double (heavy) cream

2 tbsp dill, finely chopped

Good squeeze of lemon juice

4 tsp trout roe, optional

Sea salt and freshly ground black pepper

For the garlic toasts

4 slices of sourdough bread

1 garlic clove, halved

Extra virgin olive oil, for drizzling

1. Heat the oil in a lidded sauté pan over a highish heat. Season the fish and fry for 2–3 minutes until golden, then flip over and cook on the other side for a further 2–3 minutes. Transfer to a warmed plate and keep warm in a low oven.

2. Add the clams to the pan, along with the wine. Cover and cook over a high heat for 3–4 minutes until all the clams are opened (discard any that remain closed).

3. Meanwhile, make the garlic toasts. Toast the bread, then rub it with garlic and drizzle with extra virgin olive oil.

4. Come back to the pan. Scoop out the clams with a slotted spoon into a warm bowl. Add the peas and spinach to the pan and cook until the spinach is wilted, then add the cream, dill and lemon juice.

5. Season to taste, then return the clams to the pan and stir through. Divide them between four warmed bowls and top each with a piece of fish. Drizzle with extra virgin olive oil and spoon over some trout roe. Add a good grinding of fresh black pepper and serve with the garlic toasts.

Serves 4   DF GF

Prep time: 10 minutes

Cook time: 30 minutes

Tip:

IF YOU DON'T HAVE A PRESSURE COOKER, YOU CAN MAKE THIS IN A LARGE PAN AND SIMMER GENTLY, COVERED, FOR 1½ HOURS. THE KEY HERE IS TO BLAST THE ONION, GARLIC, GINGER AND SPICES WITH PLENTY OF HEAT TO MAKE THEM AROMATIC BEFORE THEY TRANSFORM THE LIQUID. IF YOU HAVE A GAS HOB, USE KITCHEN TONGS AND CHAR THE ONION AND GINGER, WITH THEIR SKINS ON, DIRECTLY OVER THE FLAME.

Pressure Cooker Rotisserie Chicken Pho

It's hard not to fall in love with Vietnamese food culture, particularly in Hanoi, the capital city. I loved the informality of eating there: the little plastic stools and tables adorned with condiments and herbs, and in the midst of them, the food itself taking centre stage, made by a cook who had been perfecting their particular dish for years. The very first thing I tried upon our arrival to Hanoi was a big bowl of beef pho, the traditional Vietnamese soup that has now become popular around the world. Unashamedly, this recipe is a cheat's version, made with a rotisserie chicken in a pressure cooker (gasp!) to create a speedy home-cooked version of a rich and flavourful broth.

1 rotisserie chicken

1 onion, quartered

3cm (1¼in) piece of fresh ginger, sliced

2 garlic cloves

1 star anise

3 cloves

1 tsp coriander seeds

1.75 litres (7 cups) water

1 chicken stock cube

1 tbsp fish sauce

200g (7oz) folded flat rice noodles

For the toppings

1 banana shallot, thinly sliced

Large bunch of coriander (cilantro), leaves picked

2 bunches of holy basil, leaves picked

Bunch of mint, leaves picked

1 red chilli, thinly sliced

150g (5oz) beansprouts

Sriracha or hoisin sauce, for drizzling

1. Strip the meat from the rotisserie chicken, then shred and set aside. Put your pressure cooker inner pot on the hob over a medium heat and add the onion, ginger, garlic and spices. Cook in the dry pan until the onions start to catch, then add the chicken bones, water, stock cube and fish sauce.

2. Transfer the pot to the pressure cooker, set the pressure to high and cook for 20 minutes.

3. Meanwhile, cook the noodles in boiling water for 3 minutes, then drain and run under warm water to stop them sticking. Divide between four large bowls.

4. Once the stock is cooked, strain and pour over the noodles. Top with the shredded chicken and the toppings and serve.

Serves 4   V

Prep time: 5 minutes,
plus chilling

Cook time: 20 minutes

Gochujang Butter Fried Rice

If you have excitedly bought a tub of gochujang, that rather addictive fermented Korean chilli paste, but run out of things to make with it, try this. Firstly, I will say that the tub in my fridge is a regular staple ingredient, and dollops of it make their way into so many dishes. I love it slathered on roasted sweet potatoes with sesame oil, or in a great crispy Korean fried chicken bun. This particular dish is best made with cold cooked rice, so follow the cooking instructions and chill until needed – or make life easy and only make it when you have leftover rice from another meal.

250g (9oz) basmati rice

2 garlic cloves, grated

30g (1oz) salted butter

1 tbsp gochujang

200g (7oz) Tenderstem broccoli, stalks chopped into small pieces

1 tbsp sesame oil

75ml (⅓ cup) groundnut (peanut) or vegetable oil

4 medium free-range eggs

1–2 tbsp soy sauce (to taste)

4 spring onions (scallions), thinly sliced

1 red chilli, finely chopped

Salt

Drizzle of oyster sauce, to serve

Handful of coriander (cilantro) leaves, to serve

1. Rinse the rice, then tip into a saucepan and cover with 500ml (2 cups) cold water. Season with salt, cover and bring to the boil, then reduce the heat and simmer gently for 8 minutes. Remove from the heat and leave to stand with the lid on to steam for 2–3 minutes more. Fluff up with a fork. Spread out on a metal baking sheet to cool quickly. If you have time, chill for half an hour.

2. Mash the garlic and butter together with the gochujang.

3. Place a large non-stick frying pan (skillet) over a high heat and add the broccoli and a splash of water. Cover and steam for 2 minutes, then uncover and continue to cook until all the water has evaporated.

4. Add the sesame oil to the broccoli pan, then add the cold rice and fry until piping hot. Add the gochujang butter and toss well to coat.

5. Meanwhile, heat the groundnut or vegetable oil in a second frying pan over a high heat. Break in the eggs; they will puff up and go crispy around the edges. Cook until they are set to your preference, and then remove with a slotted spoon and drain on a plate lined with kitchen paper.

6. Add the soy sauce and most of the spring onions to the rice and toss together, then divide into four bowls and top each with an egg. Scatter over the chilli and remaining spring onions and finish with a drizzle of oyster sauce and some coriander leaves.

Serves 4   DF

Prep time: 5 minutes

Cook time: 15 minutes

Prawn Pil Pil Pasta

Recipes like this one make me accept I am a glutton. Fat prawns cooked in copious amounts of oil and spices are an indulgence as they are, with wedges of sourdough bread to soak up the delicious sauce – but add pasta to that mix, and you have an insight into all I love. Embrace the instant gratification this supper provides, particularly if you can get your hands on some beautiful prawns.

350g (12oz) linguine

100ml (scant ½ cup) extra virgin olive oil

150g (5oz) cherry tomatoes

3 fat garlic cloves, thinly sliced

1 tsp smoked sweet paprika

Generous pinch of chilli flakes

500g (1lb 2oz) peeled raw king prawns (jumbo shrimp)

75g (3oz) rocket (arugula) leaves

Handful of flat-leaf parsley, finely chopped

Squeeze of lemon juice

Sea salt and freshly ground black pepper

1. Bring a large pan of salted water to the boil and cook the pasta for 10–12 minutes until al dente.

2. Meanwhile, heat the oil in a large frying pan (skillet) over a medium heat and add the tomatoes. Cook gently until they start to burst, then add the garlic, paprika and chilli flakes and cook for a couple of minutes more.

3. Add the prawns, increase the heat and fry until they are pink all over. Season well with salt and pepper.

4. Drain the pasta, saving a splash of cooking water. Tip the pasta and reserved cooking water into the pan with the prawns. Toss well with the rocket leaves and parsley, squeeze over some lemon juice and serve.

Serves 4   GF

Prep time: 15 minutes

Cook time: 30 minutes

Pork Medallions with Caramelised Onion & Mustard Sauce

Pork loin fillet is a fairly versatile cut that I use regularly in stir-fries, thinly sliced and flash-fried in a hot wok. When cut into thicker medallions and simmered gently in a creamy Dijon mustard sauce, it can deservedly be the centrepiece of a quick yet sophisticated midweek dinner. Use a potato ricer for the lightest, fluffiest mashed potatoes. I have an old one I bought from a second-hand shop in Sweden that gets pulled out of the cupboard for making gnocchi and this very recipe – I often curse it, as its big steel lever means it doesn't fit perfectly anywhere, but it makes the best mashed potatoes you will ever try.

2 tbsp olive oil

500g (1lb 2oz) pork loin fillet, sliced into 1.5cm (⅔in) medallions

Good knob of salted butter

2 red onions, thinly sliced

1 tbsp apple cider vinegar

1 tbsp maple syrup

12 sage leaves

4 sprigs of thyme, leaves stripped

125ml (½ cup) white wine

200ml (generous ¾ cup) chicken stock

1 tsp Dijon mustard

Handful of flat-leaf parsley, chopped (optional)

Sea salt and freshly ground black pepper

For the garlic mash

800g (1lb 12oz) floury potatoes, cut into chunks

4 garlic cloves, peeled

30g (1oz) salted butter, plus more as needed to taste

Splash of milk

70ml (⅓ cup) double (heavy) cream

For the broccoli

300g (10oz) Tenderstem broccoli

1 tbsp olive oil

2 tbsp capers, drained and patted dry

2 tsp apple cider vinegar

2 tbsp extra virgin olive oil

1. Put the potatoes and garlic for the mash into a pan of cold salted water. Bring to the boil and simmer gently for 15 minutes.

2. Meanwhile, heat the oil in a large frying pan (skillet) over a high heat. Season the pork medallions and fry until they brown evenly on both sides, then set aside on a plate. Reduce the heat and add the butter to the pan, followed by the onions. Fry for 10 minutes until very tender. Add the apple cider vinegar, maple syrup, sage and thyme, then season well and cook for a further 5 minutes.

3. Return the pork to the pan, then add the wine and bubble for 1 minute to reduce a little. Now stir in the stock and mustard and simmer gently for 5–6 minutes until the pork is tender and cooked through.

4. Drain and mash the potatoes and garlic with the butter, milk and cream. Season well.

5. Cook the broccoli in boiling water for 2 minutes, then drain. Heat the oil in a small pan over a high heat and fry the capers until crispy, then drain on kitchen paper. Whisk the vinegar with some seasoning, then whisk in the extra virgin olive oil. Pour this over the broccoli and top with the crispy capers.

6. Scatter the pork with the parsley, then serve with the creamy garlic mash and broccoli.

Gnocchi Cacio e Pepe with Mushrooms & Sage

A quick-fix dish that is only as delicious as the quality of the ingredients you make it with. To start with, a good selection of mushrooms makes a huge difference. I've suggested an amount, but really you want to fill your pan with plenty of them of varying shapes and sizes, as they significantly reduce during the cooking time. These meaty mushroomy morsels and tender gnocchi, combined with a glossy cacio e pepe-style sauce laden with Pecorino and freshly cracked black pepper, are all you need for a dinner that really does only take minutes to make.

1–3 tsp black peppercorns (to taste)

120g (4oz) salted butter

300g (10oz) mixed mushrooms, sliced or torn

10 sage leaves

Sea salt

250g (9oz) fresh gnocchi

100g (3½oz) Parmesan cheese (or vegetarian alternative), finely grated, plus extra to serve

50g (2oz) Pecorino cheese (or vegetarian alternative), finely grated

1. Toast the peppercorns in a large, hot, dry frying pan (skillet) over a medium heat until fragrant, then roughly crush in a pestle and mortar and set aside.

2. Add 50g (2oz) of the butter to the frying pan and return to the heat. Once the butter is melted, add the mushrooms and sage leaves and fry, without stirring, for a few minutes until golden, then turn and fry on the other side for a few minutes more. Keep frying until the mushrooms are all golden. Season well, then scoop out on to a plate.

3. Bring a large pan of salted water to the boil. Add the gnocchi and cook for 2–3 minutes until they float to the surface. Scoop out with a slotted spoon and save 200ml (generous ¾ cup) of the cooking liquid.

4. Add the rest of butter to the pan you cooked the mushrooms in; once it's melted, add the toasted ground peppercorns. Stir through the reserved pasta water and simmer for a minute or so until reduced by about half.

5. Add the drained gnocchi to the pan and toss to coat in the sauce. Simmer for a minute or two, then remove from the heat and stir through the mushrooms and the cheese.

6. Serve straight away in wide bowls, with a little more Parmesan scattered over the top.

Serves 4–6

Prep time: 15 minutes

Cook time: 40 minutes

Vodka Penne Sausage Ragu

My original vodka penne recipe appeared in my second book and very first TV show back in 2011, and over the years I have made a habit of revisiting it. The sign of a good recipe is always that it stands the test of time, and while I didn't come up with the concept of sloshing vodka into tomatoes to make a creamy sauce, it's a dish my friends and family always associate with eating at mine. The loose theory behind the vodka is that it adds clarity and intensifies the sweetness of the other ingredients like the tomatoes. Whatever the case may be, I rarely ever make this without a splash of the strong stuff; in this rich version, I use pork sausages to help make a rich – almost cheat's – ragu (of sorts).

1 tbsp olive oil

500g (1lb 2oz) sausages, meat removed from skin

2 tsp fennel seeds, lightly crushed

Good pinch of chilli flakes

2 garlic cloves, thinly sliced

4 tbsp vodka

400g (14oz) tin chopped tomatoes

1 tbsp tomato purée (paste)

200ml (generous ¾ cup) chicken stock

350g (12oz) penne pasta

150ml (5fl oz) double (heavy) cream

250g (9oz) baby spinach

40g (1½oz) Parmesan cheese, finely grated

Large handful of basil leaves, to serve

Sea salt and freshly ground black pepper

1. Heat the oil in a large sauté pan (skillet) over a medium heat. Add the sausage meat and use a wooden spoon to break it up into smaller pieces. Fry for 6–8 minutes until golden brown. Add the fennel seeds, chilli flakes and garlic, and fry for a few more minutes.

2. Splash in the vodka, followed by the tomatoes, tomato purée and chicken stock. Stir to combine and simmer for 15–20 minutes until the sauce has reduced a little.

3. Bring a large pan of salted water to the boil and cook the pasta for 10 minutes until just tender. Drain, reserving a splash of cooking water.

4. Add the cream and cooking water to the ragu and simmer for a further 10 minutes, then stir in the spinach until just wilted. Check the seasoning.

5. Serve the pasta with the ragu and finish with a good scattering of Parmesan, freshly ground black pepper and the basil leaves.

Serves 4

Prep time: 10 minutes

Cook time: 8 minutes

Gnocchi al Limone with Courgette, Peas & Prawns

If there is one kitchen cupboard cheat ingredient I think is most underrated, it's a packet of gnocchi. Sure, they might not have the pillowy softness that you can achieve when you make them from scratch, but if you are stuck for time, gnocchi cooks in a matter of minutes in a pan of boiling water. As a result, I have plenty of gnocchi recipes up my sleeve for speedy suppers. This one takes all that is wonderful about creamy '*al limone*' pasta and uses prawns, courgette and frozen peas to make it dinner-worthy. Hold the Parmesan unless you really want to upset your Italian friends (though I won't judge…).

1 tbsp olive oil

Generous knob of salted butter

2 garlic cloves, thinly sliced

200g (7oz) raw king prawns (jumbo shrimp), roughly chopped

1 large courgette (zucchini), grated or julienned

1 tsp chilli flakes

Zest of 2 lemons

150g (5oz) frozen peas

450g (1lb) fresh gnocchi

100ml (scant ½ cup) double (heavy) cream

30g (1oz) Parmesan cheese, finely grated

Good handful of basil leaves

Sea salt

1. Bring a large pan of salted water to the boil for the gnocchi.

2. Heat the oil and butter in a frying pan (skillet) over a medium heat and add the garlic. Fry for 1 minute, then add the prawns and fry until turning pink. Add the courgette, chilli flakes, lemon zest and frozen peas, and stir to combine.

3. Cook the gnocchi in the boiling water for 1–2 minutes, or until they float to the surface. Scoop out of the water with a slotted spoon and add straight into the courgette and prawn pan.

4. Add the cream and Parmesan and bubble together for 1 minute, then spoon into bowls. Sprinkle with basil leaves and serve.

Serves 4 V

Prep time: 5 minutes

Cook time: 15 minutes

Green Orecchiette with Lots of Pecorino

While filming a TV series across Italy in 2013, I spent the last days of our shoot in Puglia. Despite a warm welcome in so many other regions of the country, I really fell in love with the people and food of the south. The streets of Bari are known for their pasta-making nonnas, who have become something of a tourist attraction. Many a TV host has filmed there and been challenged to make orecchiette, the region's most famous pasta shape. Despite watching the masters at work as they fired off the little ears of dough with the back of a table knife at lightning speed, I of course failed miserably to keep up when the camera was turned on me. The dough is rolled into a long snake shape before being rapidly cut and shaped to orecchione (a larger version of orecchiette), cavetelli (a smaller, tighter version) and orecchiette, the classic and most popular shape of the region.

300g (10oz) orecchiette pasta

200g (7oz) baby spinach

100g (3½oz) curly kale

3 tbsp extra virgin olive oil

2 garlic cloves, crushed

Good pinch of chilli flakes

2 tbsp crème fraîche

Squeeze of lemon juice

50g (2oz) grated Pecorino cheese (or vegetarian alternative)

Sea salt and freshly ground black pepper

1. Cook the pasta in a saucepan of salted boiling water for 10–12 minutes, or until al dente.

2. Meanwhile, blanch the spinach and kale in a saucepan of unsalted boiling water, then drain (reserving a cup of the water) and refresh under cold water. Blitz with a hand blender with a little of the cooking water until smooth.

3. Heat the oil in a frying pan (skillet) over a low heat and gently warm the garlic and chilli flakes for 1 minute. Drain the pasta and tip into the pan, then add the green purée and crème fraîche, along with a splash more of the spinach water. Add a good squeeze of lemon juice and half the grated cheese, and season to taste. Serve with the rest of the grated Pecorino and some more freshly ground black pepper.

Serves 4   DF

Prep time: 10 minutes

Cook time: 10 minutes

Joy on York Dan Dan Noodles

The neighbourhood of Highland Park was where we spent most of our weekends in Los Angeles. A favourite place to meet and eat with friends was Joy on York, a Taiwanese fast-casual dining room that had plenty to get excited about. I rarely deviated from an order of their Thousand Layer pancakes with egg, cheese, chilli and basil, a take on the Taiwanese street-food classic. It's filthy and fabulous, and the type of street food I dream of late on a Friday night in Ireland after a few negronis when the kids have been put to bed. Our regular order included mapo tofu, shrimp wontons bathed in chilli oil and piled high with chopped coriander, and their dan dan noodles, which I do my best to recreate at home.

1 tbsp groundnut (peanut) or vegetable oil

300g (10oz) minced (ground) pork

1 tsp Chinese five-spice

1 heaped tbsp hoisin sauce

1 tbsp Shaoxing rice wine

2 tbsp soy sauce

200g (7oz) leafy Asian greens, shredded

450g (10oz) medium or thick white noodles

60g (2¼oz) roasted peanuts, chopped

6 spring onions (scallions), thinly sliced

For the sauce

3 tbsp peanut butter

1 tbsp chilli oil

1 tsp Sichuan peppercorns

2 garlic cloves, thinly sliced

2 tsp caster (superfine) sugar

1. In a small bowl, mix all the ingredients for the sauce together and set aside.

2. Heat the oil in a frying pan (skillet) over a high heat and fry the minced pork until browned all over, then add the five-spice, hoisin sauce, rice wine and soy sauce. Add the greens and cover with a lid, then leave to steam for 1–2 minutes.

3. Meanwhile, cook the noodles according to packet instructions (normally in boiling water for 2–3 minutes).

4. Divide the sauce between four bowls, then drain the noodles, add to the bowls and toss with the sauce before topping with the mince and greens. Scatter with the peanuts and spring onions and serve.

Serves 4 V DF

Prep time: 15 minutes

Cook time: 25 minutes

Tip:

TO GET A REALLY GOOD CRUST ON YOUR TOFU, RESIST THE TEMPTATION TO STIR IT: JUST TURN THE CUBES AFTER EACH SIDE GETS NICE AND GOLDEN.

Mushroom & Tofu Rice Bowl

A staple quick-fix vegetarian supper in our house that requires only a handful of core ingredients. I tend to rely on a rice cooker quite a lot on hectic midweek evenings; knowing it's on and taking care of itself allows me the time to build a meal around cooked rice, but you can make this without one! If you are making this for children or for anyone who isn't a fan of spice, you can leave out the gochujang paste.

250g (9oz) basmati rice

2 tbsp groundnut (peanut) or vegetable oil

250g (9oz) firm tofu, cubed and patted dry

1 tsp sesame oil

300g (10oz) mixed oyster and shiitake mushrooms, sliced

2 garlic cloves, thinly sliced

300g (10oz) Tenderstem or purple-sprouting broccoli

For the sauce

1 tbsp sesame oil

1 tbsp gochujang paste

5 tbsp soy sauce

2 tbsp rice vinegar

2 tsp runny honey

2 tbsp toasted sesame seeds

1. Cook the rice in a saucepan of boiling salted water for 10 minutes until just tender, then drain. Return to the pan, cover with a lid and leave to steam dry.

2. Meanwhile, make the sauce: mix together all the ingredients in a small bowl and set aside.

3. Heat half the groundnut oil in a frying pan (skillet) over a medium heat and fry the tofu until golden on all sides. Tip on to a plate, then add the remaining groundnut oil and the sesame oil to the pan. Add

the mushrooms and garlic and fry over a highish heat, without stirring, until the mushrooms are tender and starting to crisp, then stir and cook for a few minutes more.

4. Steam the broccoli in a separate pan, then add to the pan with the mushrooms. Add the tofu and toss gently to warm through.

5. Divide the rice between four bowls. Top with the mushrooms, tofu and broccoli, and drizzle with the sauce.

Serves 4   DF

Prep time: 5 minutes

Cook time: 10 minutes

Pot Sticker Bowls

Tip:

IF YOU WANT TO GIVE YOUR POT STICKERS THOSE LITTLE CRISPY WINGS, MIX 60ML (¼ CUP) WATER WITH 1 TEASPOON EACH CORNFLOUR (CORNSTARCH) AND PLAIN (ALL-PURPOSE) FLOUR, A PINCH OF SALT AND ¼ TEASPOON RICE VINEGAR. ONCE YOUR POTSTICKERS HAVE BROWNED ON THE BOTTOM, POUR IN THE CORNFLOUR MIX (INSTEAD OF THE WATER), COVER WITH A LID AND COOK FOR 3-4 MINUTES. UNCOVER AND COOK FOR A MINUTE MORE UNTIL THE WINGS ARE CRISPY. TIP ON TO A PLATE AND BREAK UP, THEN SERVE AS IN THE RECIPE.

Frozen dumplings are a great standby to have in your freezer for fast but impressive lunches and dinners. Any visit to an Asian grocery store and you will find them in my basket, alongside whatever interesting-looking greens I can get my hands on, and a collection of bottles and jars that you won't find in other shops. It's always worth exploring! Furikake is another great condiment to add to your store cupboard; it's a combination of sesame seeds, seaweed and bonito flakes, and packs a serious umami punch. Sprinkle over noodles, rice, soup or even popcorn.

5 spring onions (scallions), finely shredded into long strips

1 tbsp sesame oil

24 frozen pork, chicken or prawn dumplings

2 fat garlic cloves, sliced

500g (1lb 2oz) Asian greens (pak choi, tat soi, choi sum, etc.), shredded

2 large carrots, julienned

1 cucumber, julienned

Furikake seasoning, to sprinkle (optional)

For the dressing

4 tbsp soy sauce

2 tbsp black rice or rice vinegar

1 tsp caster (superfine) sugar

1 tsp sesame oil

1. Make the dressing by mixing everything together in a bowl; set aside.

2. Put the spring onions into a bowl of cold water with some ice cubes, then set aside.

3. Drizzle half the oil into a large frying pan (skillet) over a medium–high heat. Add the dumplings, flat-side down, and cook for 1–2 minutes, then pour in 100ml (scant ½ cup) boiling water, cover and steam for 2–3 minutes.

4. Meanwhile, heat the rest of the sesame oil in a separate frying pan over a high heat and fry the garlic and greens for 1 minute. Add a little splash of water to create some steam and help them cook.

5. Divide the greens between four bowls, then add the carrot and cucumber strips. Top with the dumplings, then drizzle over the dressing or use it as a dipping sauce. Serve scattered with the now curly spring onions and a good amount of furikake seasoning.

Serves 4

Prep time: 10 minutes

Cook time: 15 minutes

Cauliflower Mac 'n' Cheese with Chorizo Crumbs

Since the arrival of children, I have attempted to include some form of nutrition in my more indulgent recipes. This one fits the bill. Lush, cheese-laden white sauce coats freshly cooked pasta; served as it is, it's pretty perfect, though I do highly recommend the chorizo crumbs. If you don't have any old bread knocking around, I often have a pack of panko breadcrumbs at the back of the kitchen cupboard, which are an ideal substitute. I've suggested using three cheeses, the combination of which yields a particularly luxurious sauce; great if you have them all, but use just one, some, or whatever you may have in the fridge.

250g (9oz) macaroni or other short pasta

1 medium cauliflower, grated with a box grater

30g (1oz) salted butter

30g (1oz) plain (all-purpose) flour

400ml (1¾ cups) whole milk

Good grating of nutmeg

60g (2¼oz) grated Gruyère

60g (2¼oz) grated mozzarella

75g (3oz) grated Cheddar

Sea salt and freshly ground black pepper

For the chorizo crumbs

1 tbsp olive oil

1 garlic clove, bashed

100g (3½oz) cured chorizo, diced small

85g (3¼oz) day-old sourdough bread, blitzed to crumbs in a food processor

Flaky sea salt

Handful of chopped flat-leaf parsley

1. For the crumbs, heat the oil in a frying pan (skillet) over a low heat and gently fry the garlic for 1 minute. Add the chorizo, increase the heat to medium and cook for 3–4 minutes until golden. Add the breadcrumbs and fry until both the bread and chorizo are golden and crispy. Drain on a plate lined with kitchen paper before sprinkling with flaky sea salt and tossing through the parsley.

2. Meanwhile, cook the pasta in a saucepan of boiling salted water for 10 minutes, adding the cauliflower for the last minute. Drain, reserving 100ml (scant ½ cup) of the cooking water.

3. Add the butter to the saucepan, followed by the flour, and cook for a couple of minutes over a medium heat before gradually stirring in the whole milk until you have a smooth, rich sauce.

4. Add a good grating of nutmeg and the grated cheeses, and allow to bubble for a few minutes until smooth and rich. Check the seasoning, then mix in the pasta and cauliflower, along with enough of the reserved cooking water to loosen.

5. Spoon into bowls and serve with the chorizo crumbs scattered over the top.

115

Slow Weekend Cooking

1. Rosemary & Thyme Confit Chicken with 20 Garlic Cloves
2. Rolled Chicken Breast with Stuffing, Roasted Veg & Pan Sauce
3. Grannie's Lamb Shoulder Recipe
4. Sticky Soy Pork Sliders with Chilli & Coriander
5. Family Focaccia-Style Pizza
6. Reverse-Seared Cote de Boeuf with Aioli & Chipped Potatoes
7. Sticky Sriracha & Ginger Popcorn Chicken with Rice & Slaw
8. Chicken Satay with Sticky Rice & Steamed Pak Choi
9½ Citrusy Harissa BBQ Lamb with Charred Greens
10. Roast Brill with Brown Butter
11. Lemony Chicken Legs with Herby Yoghurt & Crispy Crushed Pots
12. Mustard Roast Rib of Beef
13. Roasted Squash Platter with Garlic Yoghurt & Chermoula
14. Gochujang Slow-Roast Chicken
15. French Market Chicken Sunday Lunch
16. Amatriciana Meatballs
17. Slow-Roasted Pork Shoulder with Honey & Apple Vinegar Sauce

Serves 4–6 DF GF

Prep time: 20 minutes, plus chilling and marinating

Cook time: 3½ hours

Rosemary & Thyme Confit Chicken with 20 Garlic Cloves

Tip:

YOU CAN EASILY SLICE THE POTATOES HASSELBACK-STYLE BY PLACING THEM IN THE BOWL OF A WOODEN SPOON. THE EDGES OF THE SPOON WILL PREVENT YOU SLICING ALL THE WAY THROUGH: BE SURE NOT TO USE A FANCY WOODEN SPOON, THOUGH, AS IT WILL LEAVE MARKS.

Many food writers have put their stamp on chicken roasted with cloves of garlic. Nigella uses 40, Delia uses 30, but in this confit baked version of the dish, I've gone down a slightly less excessive route and settled on an easy 20 – as a result, you won't be cursing me while you're peeling them all. Chicken legs are coddled in a low oven with olive oil infused with herbs, lemon zest and garlic. It leaves you with irresistible chicken and a stellar oil that is ideal to use on roast potatoes or for frying off vegetable fritters in a pan. This recipe takes a few days to finish, so be prepared!

8 whole chicken legs (bone in and skin on)

2 sprigs of rosemary, needles stripped

5 sprigs of thyme, leaves stripped

Pared zest of 1 lemon

20 garlic cloves (about 2 whole bulbs), peeled

12 small shallots, peeled

6 baby leeks, trimmed

1 litre extra virgin olive oil

Sea salt and freshly ground black pepper

For the hasselback potatoes

800g (1lb 12oz) small/medium Desiree or Rooster potatoes or other red skinned potatoes

2 tbsp olive oil

Flaky sea salt

For the bitter leaf salad

2 heads of chicory (endive), leaves separated

1 frisée lettuce, roughly torn

1 tbsp white wine vinegar

3 tbsp of the reserved confit oil

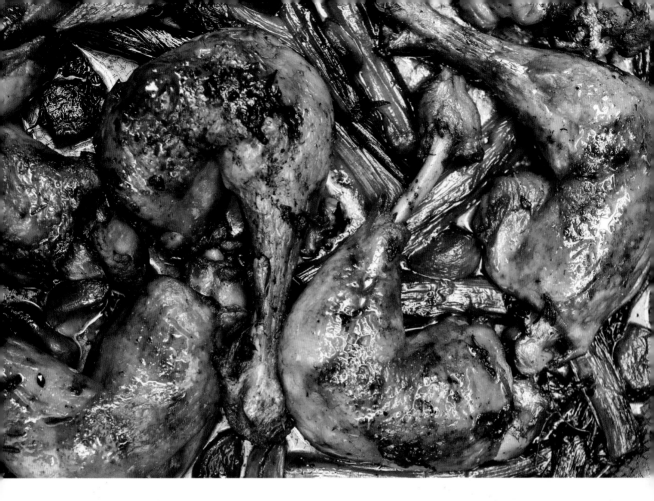

1. Place the chicken legs in a large ovenproof dish. Sprinkle over the rosemary and thyme leaves, followed by the lemon zest, garlic cloves and a generous seasoning of salt and pepper. Massage into the legs, then cover and chill overnight.

2. Preheat the oven to 150°C/130°C fan/300°F/Gas 2. Take the chicken out of the fridge and turn all the legs so they are skin-side up in the dish. Nestle the shallots and leeks in and around them, then pour over the extra virgin olive oil, making sure everything is well covered.

3. Place in the oven and cook, uncovered, for 2–2½ hours, or until the chicken is almost falling off the bone. Remove from the oven and allow to cool in the oil, preferably overnight. Once the oil is cooled completely, strain into a resealable jar and keep in the fridge for other uses.

4. Prepare your potatoes: cut small slits all the way along the length of your spuds, but not all the way through (see Tip), then massage all over with oil. Place in a roasting tray and scatter with flaky sea salt.

5. Preheat the oven to 180°C/160°C fan/350°F/Gas 4. Roast the potatoes for 40 minutes, then increase the heat to 220°C/200°C fan/425°F/Gas 7.

6. Put the chicken, shallots and leeks on to a roasting tray. Roast for about 20 minutes until the chicken skin is crispy and golden and the potatoes are golden and tender.

7. While the chicken and potatoes finish cooking in the oven, prepare the bitter leaf salad. Add the leaves to a bowl. Whisk together the white wine vinegar and reserved confit oil, then drizzle over the leaves and toss to combine. Serve with the chicken and potatoes.

Serves 4

Prep time: 30 minutes,
plus chilling

Cook time: 1 hour

Rolled Chicken Breast with Stuffing, Roasted Veg & Pan Sauce

I am not a fan of anything too fiddly when it comes to home cooking, so when I suggest bashing, rolling and searing, know that I do so with the promise of a decent payoff. There is a little effort involved in this one, but like many of the recipes I hold dear, the end results are, of course, worth it. At its core, this is a meat-and-two-veg recipe, but with a few little fancy flourishes that will make you shine if you serve it for a dinner party. I made this with Sarah Hughes in Howth Castle, where she runs a brilliant cookery school; we used turkey escalopes as a sort of cheat's Christmas dinner. The ballotines can be prepared in advance to make life easy.

Olive oil, for drizzling

40g (1½oz) salted butter

1 small red onion, finely chopped

2 garlic cloves, crushed

175g (6oz) stale white bread, blitzed to crumbs

8 sage leaves, finely chopped

Small handful of chopped flat-leaf parsley

1 tsp Dijon mustard

1 medium free-range egg, beaten

2 large free-range chicken breasts

10 slices of prosciutto

1 tbsp plain (all-purpose) flour

120ml (½ cup) white wine

300ml (1¼ cups) chicken stock

Sea salt and freshly ground black pepper

For the roasted veg

1kg (2lb 4oz) floury potatoes, peeled and quartered

Olive oil, for drizzling

Small handful of rosemary sprigs

450g (1lb) parsnips, peeled and sliced lengthways

450g (1lb) carrots, peeled and sliced lengthways

Small handful of thyme sprigs

Drizzle of runny honey

Continued overleaf

SLOW WEEKEND COOKING

1. Prepare your chicken up to a day ahead. Heat a drizzle of oil and the butter in a frying pan (skillet) over a medium heat and fry the onion for 10 minutes until softened, then add the garlic, breadcrumbs and sage and fry until the breadcrumbs are lightly golden but still squishy. Season well and add the parsley and mustard, then tip into a bowl to cool. Add the egg and mix with your hands.

2. Use a rolling pin to flatten the chicken breasts between two sheets of baking parchment or cling film (plastic wrap). You want to get them as thin as possible without making holes.

3. Roll out a large piece of cling film on your countertop and place 5 slices of prosciutto next to each other, slightly overlapping by about 1cm (½in). Place one of the chicken breasts on top.

4. Take half of the stuffing and arrange it in the centre of the chicken, running the length of the escalope. Roll up the meat, using the cling film to help you, to make a tight cylinder shape. Twist the ends tightly to keep it together. Repeat to make a second roll and place in the fridge to chill for at least 30 minutes.

5. Meanwhile, preheat the oven to 200°C/180°C fan/400°F/Gas 6.

6. Put the potatoes into a pan of cold salted water, then bring to the boil and simmer gently for 3–4 minutes until they start to cook on the outside. Drain and return them to the dry pan. Shake the pan gently to fluff up the edges of the potatoes.

7. Drizzle a large roasting tray generously with olive oil, making sure you cover the entire surface of the tray, and transfer to the oven for 10 minutes.

8. Once the oil is hot, place a few sprigs of rosemary in the tray, then add the potatoes. Use a spoon to gently coat the potatoes in the oil, then transfer the tray back to the oven to roast for 45 minutes until golden and crispy.

9. Meanwhile, put the carrots and parsnips in a second large roasting tray. Drizzle with 2 tablespoons of olive oil and toss with the thyme and plenty of seasoning. Roast for 45 minutes until caramelised. At this stage, take them out of the oven and drizzle with honey, before transferring back to the oven to roast for a further 10 minutes. Keep warm.

10. Halfway through the veggie cooking time, heat a little oil in an ovenproof frying pan (skillet) over a medium–high heat. Unwrap the chicken and brown all over until golden, then transfer to the oven and roast for 15–20 minutes. Set aside on a warm plate or board to rest while you make the pan gravy.

11. Put the pan over a lowish heat and add the flour to the roasting juices. Cook for 1 minute, then pour in the wine and bubble for a further couple of minutes before adding the stock. Simmer gently until you have a gravy-like consistency, then season to taste.

12. To serve, slice the chicken and serve with the roast potatoes, carrots and parsnips, and a generous drizzle of the pan sauce.

Serves 6   GF

Prep time: 20 minutes

Cook time: 3½–4 hours

Grannie's Lamb Shoulder

One of my earliest memories of my grannie's cooking was snaffling some of her famous roast lamb out of a tin foil package in the back seat of my mom's car. I'd been hanging around the kitchen on one of our regular Sunday visits and had been soaking up the tantalising smells of lamb shoulder slow-cooking in the oven. As we were leaving, she pressed the warm tin foil package into my hand and sent me on my way. Even now, when I carve a roast leg of lamb and dip the crusty best bits in flaky salt, it's a taste that instantly reminds me of her. Salty, rosemary-laden slices of lamb and the smell of home.

2kg (4lb 8oz) whole shoulder of lamb

2 sprigs of rosemary, needles stripped

2 garlic cloves, thinly sliced

Sea salt and freshly ground black pepper

For the boulangère potatoes

50g (2oz) salted butter

2 large onions, thinly sliced

1.5kg (3lb 5oz) Desiree potatoes (or other large slightly waxy potatoes), peeled and thinly sliced

10 sage leaves, thinly sliced

400ml (1¾ cups) chicken stock

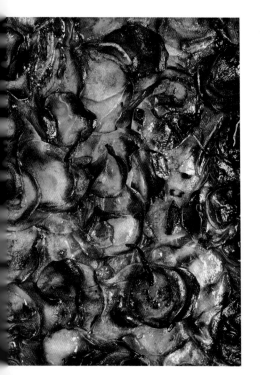

1. Preheat the oven to 160°C/140°C fan/320°F/Gas 3. Take your shoulder of lamb and use a sharp knife to make small incisions all over the meat. Push little bits of rosemary and slices of garlic into the cuts, then season well all over.

2. Rub a large ovenproof dish with half the butter. Layer up the sliced onions, potatoes and sage leaves, seasoning well in between each layer, then pour over the chicken stock and dot with the remaining butter.

3. Put the potatoes into the oven, with the lamb sitting on a wire rack directly above the potatoes so the meaty juices drip down into the potatoes below.

4. Slow-roast for 3–3½ hours until the meat is really tender, then increase the temperature to 220°C/200°C fan/425°F/Gas 7 for a further 20 minutes so the meat is lovely and brown and the potatoes golden. Let them both rest for 10 minutes before serving.

Serves 6   DF

Prep time: 20 minutes

Cook time: 2 hours 40 minutes

Sticky Soy Pork Sliders with Chilli & Coriander

There are many cuts of meat that benefit from the low-and-slow treatment, but perhaps none more than the ubiquitous pork belly. It may have had its day on restaurant menus, but it's a rewarding and inexpensive cut for the home cook. Take inspiration from Chinese pantry ingredients and you won't go too far wrong; the fatty, tender meat is best infused with salty soy, rice wine and fresh aromatics like ginger and garlic. After the cut has been anointed and slowly baked, the sticky slices are irresistible sandwiched between pillowy brioche buns and crunchy slaw. Certainly one for a weekend treat for the whole crew!

1.2kg (2lb 10oz) piece of pork belly

12 brioche slider buns

For the cooking liquid

5 garlic cloves, sliced

5cm (2oz) piece of fresh ginger, grated

75ml (⅓ cup) soy sauce

60ml (¼ cup) Shaoxing rice wine

2 tbsp soft light brown sugar

1 red chilli, halved lengthways

1 star anise

2 tsp Sichuan peppercorns

125ml (½ cup) water

For the slaw

2 carrots

½ red cabbage

¼ white cabbage

100ml (scant ½ cup) rice vinegar

2 tbsp caster (superfine) sugar

1 tbsp sesame oil

2 tbsp sesame seeds, toasted

Large handful of coriander (cilantro) leaves, roughly torn

1. Preheat the oven to 160°C/140°C fan/320°F/Gas 3. In a jug, mix together all the ingredients for the cooking liquid. Put the pork into a roasting tray and pour over the cooking liquid. Cover tightly with foil and slow-cook for 2½ hours until very tender. Remove from the oven and pour the juices back into the jug. Allow the meat to cool completely (you can leave it to cool until the next day if you are making these sliders in advance).

2. To make the slaw, shred the carrots and cabbage and combine in a bowl. Heat the rice vinegar and caster sugar in a small saucepan over a medium heat with 2 tablespoons of water until the sugar has dissolved. Pour this mix over the shredded vegetables and set aside to macerate for at least 15 minutes. Once the slaw has macerated, add the sesame oil, sesame seeds and coriander.

3. When you are ready to serve, prepare the meat. Remove any excess skin and fat from the pork, then carve into slices. Pour or scoop off any fat from the juices reserved in the jug, then pour the juices into a large frying pan (skillet). Place over a medium heat until bubbling, then add the slices of pork belly and cook, turning, for 5–10 minutes until they are sticky and coloured. Meanwhile, lightly toast the buns.

4. Fill the buns with the sticky pork and top with the slaw. Serve with any extra slaw on the side.

Serves 6   V

Tip:

TRY THE BASIL OIL ON PAGE 34 TO DRIZZLE OVER THE TOP
BEFORE SERVING, OR MAKE A QUICK PESTO TO SPOON OVER.

Prep time: 20 minutes,
plus resting and proving

Cook time: 25-27 minutes

Family Focaccia-Style Pizza

My major takeaway from all the breadmaking that went on during the pandemic was that time changes everything. From pizza to sourdough bread and beyond, the key to making bread is the time it's left to rise. My best version of homemade pizza begins on a Thursday, with a couple of turns to the dough in the fridge over the following days before it goes into the oven. However, as I'm rarely that organised, this focaccia-style pizza is an easier option – it's a loose, no-knead dough that only requires a bit of time and minimal effort to give wonderful results. You can serve it pizza-style, like I've suggested here, or make a basil and garlic oil to rub over the surface before poking deep dimples into the dough before baking. Be sure to bake this until the edges are crisp and the centre is cooked through. The dough has a high moisture content, so does require a slightly longer cooking time.

1 x 7g (¼oz) sachet dried yeast

1 tbsp runny honey

700ml (3 cups) warm water

550g (4½ cups) '00' flour

100g (scant 1 cup) white rye flour

1 tbsp sea salt flakes, plus extra for sprinkling

5 tbsp extra virgin olive oil, plus extra for drizzling

75g (3oz) grated mozzarella

125g (4oz) ball buffalo mozzarella, torn

Handful of basil leaves, to serve

For the tomato sauce

1 tbsp extra virgin olive oil

1 garlic clove, bashed

200ml (generous ¾ cup) passata

Sea salt and freshly ground black pepper

Continued overleaf

1. Mix together the dried yeast, honey and warm water in a large bowl. Whisk, then leave for 15 minutes until a foam forms.

2. Add the flours and salt to the yeast mixture and stir to combine with a wooden spoon until you have a rough but evenly mixed dough; it will be very loose.

3. Add 3 tablespoons of the extra virgin olive oil to a separate large, clean bowl and transfer the dough into this. Turn to coat the dough in the oil, then cover and leave in the fridge overnight (alternatively, leave covered at room temperature for 4 hours if you want to bake the same day).

4. Keeping the dough in the bowl, lightly coat your hands with oil and pull up the edge of the dough, then fold over the top. Repeat this on all four sides, turning the bowl a quarter turn each time to make this easier. Do this three times in total.

5. Add the remaining 2 tablespoons of oil to a 38 x 25cm (15 x 10in) baking tray that is at least 2cm (¾in) deep. Gently press the dough into the tray, spreading it out to the edges. Leave to rise for at least an hour at room temperature, uncovered.

6. While this is rising, make the tomato sauce. Heat the oil in a deep pan (to prevent splattering), then add the garlic and cook for 1 minute. Stir in the passata, season well and simmer for 5–6 minutes until reduced and thickened.

7. Preheat the oven to 220°C/200°C fan/425°F/Gas 7.

8. You will know your dough is ready when you poke it and the indentation slowly springs back but still leaves an impression. Oil your hands and then, to create the characteristic indentations, spread your fingers apart and press them into the dough, reaching the base of the tray.

9. Drizzle with extra virgin olive oil and bake for 15 minutes until lightly golden, then spread evenly with the tomato sauce and scatter over the grated mozzarella and torn buffalo mozzarella. Bake for a further 10–12 minutes, until the cheese has melted and the crusts are golden brown.

10. Leave to cool for 5 minutes, then slide a thin spatula underneath and transfer the pizza to a board to slice. Serve scattered with basil leaves.

Serves 4   GF

Prep time: 10 minutes, plus resting

Cook time: 1 hour 20 minutes

Tip:

YOU CAN COOK THE STEAKS LIKE THIS WELL IN ADVANCE – EVEN UP TO A DAY BEFORE – SO THAT ALL YOU HAVE TO DO AT THE LAST MINUTE IS FRY THEM IN THE HOT PAN. JUST REMEMBER TO REMOVE THEM FROM THE FRIDGE AND BRING THEM UP TO ROOM TEMPERATURE BEFORE YOU SEAR THEM.

Reverse-Seared Côte de Boeuf with Aioli & Chipped Potatoes

Nail your steak game with this reverse-sear method that pretty much guarantees great results, particularly when you are cooking an expensive cut of meat. A meat thermometer is essential if you want to achieve perfectly medium-rare meat. Ask your butcher to cut the meat about 3cm (1¼in) thick. Steak and homemade chips, finished off with some homemade aioli – you've got killer steak frites!

2 x single rib côte de boeuf (about 3cm/1¼in thick)

2 tbsp olive oil

60g (2¼oz) salted butter

2 garlic cloves, bashed

3 sprigs of rosemary

100g (3½oz) wild rocket (arugula) leaves

20g (¾oz) Parmesan cheese shavings

Sea salt and freshly ground black pepper

For the chipped potatoes

1kg (2lb 4oz) floury potatoes, peeled and cut into 1cm (⅓in) cubes

4 tbsp olive oil

For the aioli

1 large free-range egg yolk

1 tsp white wine vinegar

1 large garlic clove, finely grated

½ tsp Dijon mustard

100ml (scant ½ cup) olive oil

50ml (scant ¼ cup) extra virgin olive oil

1 tbsp finely chopped tarragon

Squeeze of lemon juice

Continued overleaf

1. Remove the steaks from the fridge half an hour before cooking. Season well with salt and pepper on both sides and then place on a wire rack set over a roasting tray. Leave uncovered until you are ready to cook.

2. Preheat the oven to 140°C/120°C /280°F/Gas 1. Place the steak in the oven for 25–35 minutes for medium-rare. Use a meat thermometer to test the internal temperature: it should read 55°C/130°F.

3. Meanwhile, put the potatoes into a saucepan of cold salted water and bring to the boil. Simmer for 2 minutes, then drain and return to the dry pan over a low heat; shake gently to fluff up the edges.

4. For the aioli, put the egg yolk, vinegar, garlic, Dijon mustard and a pinch of sea salt into a bowl. Whisk in both olive oils in a thin but steady stream until you have a thick mayonnaise. Add the tarragon and lemon juice to taste.

5. Once the steaks are finished in the oven, remove and allow them to sit until you are ready to sear.

6. Increase the oven temperature to 210°C/190°C fan/410°F/Gas 6. Pour the oil for the potatoes into a roasting tray and heat in the oven for a few minutes, then add the cubed potatoes, coating evenly in the oil. Roast for 40–45 minutes until golden and crisp.

7. To finish the beef, heat the oil in a heavy-based frying pan (skillet) over a high heat and add the steaks. Cook for almost 1 minute, or until nicely browned, then flip over, adding the butter, garlic and rosemary to the pan.

8. Tilt the pan and use a spoon to baste the steaks continuously for another minute. Remove the steaks from the pan and leave to rest for a few minutes, then slice, saving the resting juices in a small bowl.

9. Serve the sliced steak with the potatoes and a tumble of rocket and Parmesan on the side, with the resting juices poured over the top like a dressing.

SLOW WEEKEND COOKING

Serves 6   DF

Prep time: 30 minutes,
plus marinating

Cook time: 30 minutes

Sticky Sriracha & Ginger Popcorn Chicken with Rice & Slaw

Saturday night takeaway, home kitchen-style! The trick to crispy popcorn chicken is to use potato flour or cornflour, which will give the umami-laden nuggets the addictive crispness required. Expect this to be a regular Saturday night request.

8 skinless chicken thigh fillets, cut into bite-sized chunks

3cm (1¼in) piece of fresh ginger, peeled and grated

2 garlic cloves, grated

3 tbsp Shaoxing rice wine

2 tbsp soy sauce

200g (7oz) potato flour or cornflour (cornstarch)

1 tsp Chinese five-spice

750ml (3 cups) vegetable oil

250g (9oz) basmati rice, rinsed

1 tbsp sesame seeds, toasted

5 spring onions (scallions), thinly sliced

Sea salt

For the glaze

2 tbsp tomato ketchup

4 tbsp sriracha

2 tbsp soft dark brown sugar

2cm (¾in) piece of fresh ginger, peeled and grated

1 garlic clove, grated

2 tbsp dark soy sauce

1 tbsp toasted sesame oil

For the slaw

1 medium white cabbage, cored and finely shredded

2 large carrots, julienned

3 spring onions (scallions), thinly sliced

1 tbsp sriracha

2 tbsp rice vinegar

2 tsp fish sauce

2 tbsp soy sauce

1 tbsp soft light brown sugar

1 tbsp sesame oil

Handful of mint or Thai basil leaves

Continued overleaf

1. Put the chicken into a dish with the ginger, garlic, rice wine and soy sauce, and marinate for at least 30 minutes.

2. Preheat the oven to 220°C/200°C fan/425°F/Gas 7. Toss the flour with the five-spice in a large resealable freezer bag.

3. Heat a 5cm (2in) layer of oil in a large wok or heavy-based frying pan (skillet) over a medium heat until it is shimmering (about 170°C/340°F, or when a cube of bread browns in 45 seconds). Take the chicken pieces out of the marinade, shake off any excess, then add to the freezer bag and toss to coat all over.

4. Working in batches, fry the chicken for 2–3 minutes, turning occasionally, until golden all over. Remove from the pan, drain on kitchen paper and place on a baking sheet. Transfer to the oven and bake for 15–20 minutes.

5. Meanwhile, put all the glaze ingredients into a saucepan over a medium heat and bubble together for a minute or two, then set aside.

6. In a large bowl, mix together all the ingredients for the slaw and set aside.

7. Put the rice into a pan and cover with 500ml (2 cups) cold water. Season with salt, cover and bring to the boil, then simmer gently for 10 minutes. Remove from the heat and leave to stand with the lid on to steam for 2–3 more minutes. Fluff up with a fork.

8. Once the chicken is golden and crispy, place in bowls, drizzle all over with the glaze, scatter over the sesame seeds and spring onions, and serve with the rice and slaw.

Serves 4–6   DF

Prep time: 10 minutes,
plus marinating

Cook time: 50 minutes

Tip:

IF YOU CHILL THE TIN OF COCONUT MILK FIRST, YOU'LL
END UP WITH A NICE FIRM CREAM ON TOP TO USE FOR THE
MARINADE.

Chicken Satay with Sticky Rice & Steamed Pak Choi

Chicken satay served family-style with rice and greens makes a weekend feast to look forward to. My wife Sofie has a peanut allergy, so I sometimes make this with tahini paste in place of peanut butter and it works just as well, though I do slightly miss the rich creaminess you get from peanut butter – the price I guess I have to pay for keeping her from anaphylactic shock! The base method and sauce for this recipe work well with pieces of pork tenderloin or chunks of sweet potato if you'd prefer a vegetarian version.

8 chicken thighs (bone in and skin on)

1 tbsp groundnut (peanut) or vegetable oil

For the marinade

2 tbsp coconut cream from a 400ml (14fl oz) tin coconut milk

1 tbsp Thai red curry paste

2 tbsp peanut butter

1 tbsp fish sauce

1 tbsp soy sauce

1 tbsp soft light brown sugar

For the sauce

400ml (14fl oz) tin coconut milk (minus the 2 tbsp used in the marinade)

3 tbsp peanut butter

2 tbsp Thai red curry paste

1 tbsp fish sauce

2 tbsp soy sauce

2 tbsp soft light brown sugar

1 tbsp tamarind purée

To serve

200g (7oz) sticky rice

4 pak choi, quartered

50g (2oz) roasted peanuts, chopped

Large handful of coriander (cilantro) leaves, roughly chopped

Lime wedges

1. Put the chicken thighs into a dish. Mix together all of the marinade ingredients in a bowl, then add to the chicken and stir to coat evenly. Leave to marinate for at least 30 minutes.

2. To make the sauce, whisk all the ingredients together until smooth.

3. Place a casserole dish over a medium heat and add the oil. When shimmering, add the chicken and brown all over until sticky and dark.

4. Pour in the sauce, then reduce the heat and simmer, uncovered, for 45 minutes until the chicken is lovely and tender.

5. Meanwhile, cook the rice according to the packet instructions and steam the pak choi until tender.

6. Serve the chicken, scattered with peanuts and coriander, with the sticky rice and steamed greens along with some lime wedges to squeeze over the top.

Serves 6–8   DF GF

Prep time: 20 minutes,
plus marinating and
resting

Cook time: 40 minutes

Tip:

IF YOU WANT TO COOK THIS IN THE OVEN INSTEAD OF THE BARBECUE, PREHEAT THE OVEN TO 200°C/180°C FAN/400°F/GAS 6 AND COOK THE LAMB FOR 30 MINUTES, THEN REDUCE THE TEMPERATURE TO 160°C/140°C FAN/320°F/GAS 3 AND COOK FOR A FURTHER 1½ HOUR. COOK THE VEGGIES ON A SMOKING HOT GRIDDLE PAN FOR A DEEP SMOKY FLAVOUR. COUSCOUS, SPIKED WITH HERBS AND THINLY SLICED PRESERVED LEMON, WOULD BE AN IDEAL ADDITION TO YOUR LAMB FEAST.

Citrusy Harissa Barbecued Lamb with Charred Greens

If there's one meat I insist you cook on the barbecue, it's lamb. It's one of my favourite tastes of summer. Lamb shoulder is so spectacular grilled over hot coals; cooked to perfection, it should be blushing pink, smoky and sweet. Sliced thinly and served with this citrus-pumped harissa sauce, it's a recipe you will revisit again and again.

2kg (3lb 5oz) lamb shoulder (bone in)

For the citrusy harissa sauce

3 tbsp rose harissa paste

3 tbsp extra virgin olive oil

2 garlic cloves, finely grated

6 sprigs of thyme, leaves stripped

Zest and juice of 1 orange

Zest and juice of 1 lemon

For the charred greens

10 spring onions (scallions), trimmed

2 baby gem lettuces, quartered

4 endives (chicory), trimmed and halved

1 tbsp olive oil

1 tbsp sherry vinegar

3 tbsp extra virgin oliver oil

Sea salt and freshly ground black pepper

For the cumin salt

1 tbsp flaky sea salt

2 tsp cumin seeds, toasted

1. Whisk together the ingredients for the citrusy harissa sauce and set aside.

2. Massage the lamb with half of the citrusy harissa sauce, then leave to marinate for at least 30 minutes, or covered in the fridge overnight.

3. Prepare a barbecue to a high heat (around 220°C/430°F if you have a barbecue thermometer). If you can, use an indirect grilling technique by pushing the coals to one side of the barbecue.

4. Add the lamb to the centre of the grill, then cover and cook for 2½ hours, letting the temperature drop down to around 180°C/350°F as it cooks.

5. Just before the lamb is ready, brush the spring onions, gem lettuces and endives with the olive oil and season with salt and pepper. In a bowl, whisk the sherry vinegar with some seasoning, then gradually whisk in the extra virgin olive oil and set aside.

6. When the lamb is cooked, transfer to a chopping board with deep grooves to

catch the juices, then cover with foil and allow to rest for about 5 minutes. Place the vegetables on the barbecue and cook until charred on all sides. Remove to a plate, drizzle over the vinegar mix, and keep covered and warm.

7. To make the cumin salt, bash the salt and toasted cumin seeds together in a pestle and mortar.

8. Slice the lamb thinly and serve with the charred vegetables, a large drizzle of the remaining citrusy harissa sauce and a good sprinkle of the cumin salt.

Serves 4   GF

Prep time: 10 minutes

Cook time: 25 minutes

Roast Brill with Brown Butter

I know for many, tackling a large whole fish may seem a little daunting, but I urge you to try this beauty. Given a little love before its time in a hot oven, it becomes a true showstopper and celebration of a delicious fish to share with friends and family. The sharp, nutty, brown butter sauce makes the tender white flesh all the more delicious, while the capers add punch. If I have the pizza oven fired up, this is a lovely dish to pop in. To test if the fish is cooked, take a sharp knife and insert its tip into the fish in the thickest part, near the gills along the backbone. If the meat slides easily away from the bones when pushed with the knife, then it is cooked.

750g (1lb 10oz) new potatoes

1.5g (3lb 5oz) whole brill, cleaned

3 sprigs of rosemary, needles stripped

Pared zest of 1 lemon

60g (2¼oz) unsalted butter, plus an extra knob

90ml (generous ⅓ cup) extra virgin olive oil

2 tbsp capers

1 tbsp red wine vinegar

2 bunches of asparagus, trimmed

Handful of flat-leaf parsley, finely chopped

Sea salt and freshly ground black pepper

1. Preheat the oven to 220°C/200°C fan/425°F/Gas 7.

2. Put the potatoes into a pan of cold salted water, then bring to the boil and simmer for 15 minutes until tender.

3. Meanwhile, put the brill into a roasting tray and tuck the rosemary and lemon parings under the fish. Season well, then roast in the oven for 15–20 minutes until the fish is just cooked.

4. At the same time, melt the butter in a frying pan (skillet) and then bubble until it starts to smell nutty. Set aside.

5. Heat 2 tablespoons of the extra virgin olive oil in a small frying pan over a medium heat and fry the capers until crispy, then drain on kitchen paper. Whisk the rest of the olive oil with the red wine vinegar. Pour this over the fish and return to the oven for 5 minutes.

6. Steam the asparagus for 3 minutes until tender, then drain. Toss the asparagus and potatoes with half the brown butter and scatter over the parsley. Pour the rest of the brown butter over the brill and scatter over the crispy capers. Serve the brill with its delicious sauce and the potatoes and asparagus on the side.

Serves 4 GF

Prep time: 10 minutes

Cook time: 1 hour

Lemony Chicken Legs with Herby Yoghurt & Crispy Crushed Potatoes

I love listening to food podcasts as I cook on a Sunday: *The Splendid Table* with Lynne Rossetto Kasper and now Francis Lam, *Good Food* with Evan Kleiman, with reports from the LA food world, and, more recently, Ruth Rogers's fabulous *Table 4*, where she speaks to the most impossibly interesting people. After I've had a coffee and read the snippets of the papers, I get to work in the kitchen on a dish like this one: something where most of it can essentially be prepared in advance and then the oven takes care of the rest before we sit down for a Sunday dinner as a family. There might be time to make dessert, too, if the children aren't too feral or if I'm particularly enjoying the episode. It reminds me of listening to my own mom pottering away in the kitchen listening to *The Archers* on the radio. A family tradition passed down unknowingly.

750g (1lb 10oz) new potatoes

4 whole chicken legs

2 tsp za'atar

1 tsp Aleppo pepper flakes

Finely grated zest of 1 lemon

4 tbsp olive oil

2 tbsp capers, drained and patted dry

Sea salt and freshly ground black pepper

For the herby yoghurt

175g (6oz) Greek yoghurt

1 garlic clove, grated

Large handful of flat-leaf parsley, finely chopped

Small handful of mint leaves, finely chopped

Good squeeze of lemon juice

Sprinkling of sumac

1. Preheat the oven to 210°C/190°C fan/410°F/Gas 6½.

2. Put the potatoes into a pan of cold salted water and bring to the boil, then simmer gently for 12–15 minutes.

3. Toss the chicken pieces with the za'atar, Aleppo pepper, lemon zest and 2 tablespoons of the oil. Season well with salt and pepper.

4. Pour the rest of the oil into a large roasting tray and put into the oven to heat up. Drain the potatoes, then tumble them into the tray. Squash them down with the bottom of a glass so they spread out. Season, then nestle the chicken legs into the tray and roast for 30 minutes.

5. Add the capers to the tray, then flip the potatoes and cook for a further 15 minutes until the chicken, potatoes and capers are golden and crispy.

6. Meanwhile, put all the ingredients for the yoghurt, except the sumac, into a small food processor and whizz together. Once you have a thick green yoghurt, spoon into a bowl and sprinkle with the sumac.

7. Once the chicken is cooked, place on a platter with the potatoes and serve with the herby yoghurt.

SLOW WEEKEND COOKING

Serves 6–8

Prep time: 20 minutes

Cook time: 1½–2 hours

Mustard Roast Rib of Beef

Roast rib of beef was always saved for special occasions when I was a kid. For good reason, too; a beautiful rib of beef on the bone from the butcher's is a showstopper and deserves all the trimmings. While I didn't grow up with Yorkshire puddings (I don't know many Irish families who did), they are a recent addition to the line-up, and they provide real wow factor when they land on the table. The Irish food writer Theodora FitzGibbon has a recipe for her version of them entitled 'batter puddings', which I think are as Irish as we're going to get them to be. I've followed suit – batter puddings it is from here on out.

2 ribs of beef on the bone (approx. 1.8kg/4lb)

2 tsp black peppercorns

2 tsp white mustard seeds

2 tsp black mustard seeds

1 tbsp soft light brown sugar

½ tsp mustard powder

3 sprigs of thyme, leaves stripped

6 carrots, halved lengthways

5 parsnips, halved lengthways

3 red onions, cut into wedges

2 tbsp olive oil

1 tbsp plain (all-purpose) flour

120ml (½ cup) madeira

500ml (2 cups) beef stock

Sea salt and freshly ground black pepper

For the batter puds

150g (1¼ cups) plain (all-purpose) flour

2 medium free-range eggs

200–225ml (generous ¾ cup–scant 1 cup) milk

12 tsp beef dripping or olive oil

1. Bring the meat out of the fridge an hour before cooking to come up to room temperature.

2. Preheat the oven to 220°C/200°C fan/425°F/Gas 7. Lightly toast the peppercorns and mustard seeds in a dry frying pan (skillet) over a low heat until fragrant, then bash with a pestle and mortar and mix with the sugar, mustard powder and thyme leaves. Spread this mixture all over the beef.

3. Scatter the veggies into a large roasting tray, drizzle with the oil and season with salt and pepper, then sit the rib of beef in the middle. Roast for 20 minutes, then reduce the oven temperature to 170°C/150°C fan/340°F/Gas 3 and roast for a further 50–60 minutes for medium-rare.

4. Meanwhile, make the pudding batter. Put the flour into a bowl and make a well in the centre. Add the eggs and gradually stir the flour into the eggs, adding the milk a little at a time until you have a smooth batter about the consistency of double (heavy) cream. You may not need all the milk specified.

5. Once the beef is cooked, transfer to a warm serving plate with the veggies, saving any meat juices in the tray. Keep warm.

6. Increase the oven temp to 220°C/200°C fan/425°F/Gas 7 again. Put a little dripping or oil into the cups of a 12-hole Yorkie tin and heat in the oven until smoking. Add the batter to the hot fat in the cups, filling them not quite to the top, then return to the oven to cook for 30–35 minutes until golden and puffed.

7. Meanwhile, put the roasting tray over a low heat and stir the flour into any fat and resting juices. Add the madeira and bubble for a few minutes, then gradually whisk in the stock until you have a smooth gravy. Season to taste.

8. Slice the beef and serve with the veggies, batter puds and gravy.

SLOW WEEKEND COOKING

Serves 6   V GF

Prep time: 20 minutes

Cook time: 40 minutes

Roasted Squash Platter with Garlic Yoghurt & Chermoula

The aromas of this weekend feast will transport you to the souks of Marrakech. Ras el hanout (a potent blend of over 30 spices – salty, punchy lip-puckering preserved lemons and vibrant fresh herbs) lift sweet caramelised squash to new heights. Much of my weekend cooking and, in particular, the cooking I truly enjoy, is based around make-ahead plates that can be prepared long before the bustle of friends or family enter the kitchen. This platter of sweet roast squash is a tangle of North African spices and other good things, layered to be served as the veggie feast centrepiece.

2–3 autumn squash or pumpkins depending on size (such as Onion, Kabocha, Crown Prince, Turban or Harlequin)

1 bulb of garlic, cloves separated and skin left on

1 tsp cumin seeds

2 tsp coriander seeds

1 tsp ras el hanout

Good pinch of chilli flakes

3 tbsp olive oil

Drizzle of runny honey

400g (14oz) tin chickpeas, drained, rinsed and patted dry

50g (2oz) wild rocket (arugula) leaves

Good sprinkling of sumac

Sea salt and freshly ground black pepper

For the yoghurt

300g (10oz) natural yoghurt

1 garlic clove, crushed

1 small green chilli, finely chopped

Good squeeze of lemon juice

For the chermoula

50g (2oz) coriander (cilantro)

25g (1oz) flat-leaf parsley

3 garlic cloves, grated

2 preserved lemons, flesh discarded and skin thinly sliced (or use the finely grated zest of 2 lemons)

75–90ml (5–6 tbsp) extra virgin olive oil

½ tsp ground cumin

Pinch of hot smoked paprika

1. Preheat the oven to 200°C/180°C fan/400°F/Gas 6.

2. Slice the squash into wedges (discarding the seeds but keeping the skin on) and arrange in two large roasting trays. Scatter with the garlic cloves and spices, then toss with the oil and plenty of seasoning and roast for 20 minutes.

3. Turn the squash wedges over and drizzle with honey, then add the chickpeas and roast for a further 20 minutes until tender and golden.

4. Meanwhile, blend all the ingredients for the yoghurt together and set aside.

5. Finely chop the herbs for the chermoula and mix with the rest of the ingredients; season well and set aside.

6. When the squash is cooked, toss with the rocket leaves and sprinkle with sumac. Serve with the spiced yoghurt and chermoula.

Serves 4–6   DF

Prep time: 30 minutes

Cook time: 3 hours

Gochujang Slow-Roast Chicken

Truth be told, I am an anxious cook. Over the years I have learned that when feeding a crowd, I have my best kitchen successes with food that can be prepared well in advance. If you see me in the kitchen still bashing away at pots and pans while sipping a welcome drink, trouble is brewing. I once grabbed a hot pan directly from the oven with my bare hands during a particularly stressful meal I had chosen to test myself with. You live, you learn, you get burnt! So I do like to think I speak with experience when I suggest you choose simple dishes that are more of an assembly job when it comes to serving time. This one is a good example: you get great results with simple ingredients that can tick away in the oven while you prepare for your guests. Though just to be safe, have some burn spray on hand, in case you truly lose the run of yourself.

1.8kg (4lb) free-range chicken

1 tbsp gochujang paste

2 tbsp runny honey

2 tbsp soy sauce

2 tsp sesame oil

1 bulb of garlic, halved through the middle

5cm (2in) piece of fresh ginger, roughly chopped

1kg (2lb 4oz) sweet potatoes, cut into wedges

Good drizzle of olive oil

Large bunch of coriander (cilantro), chopped

Sea salt and freshly ground black pepper

Steamed rice, to serve

For the dipping sauce

3 tbsp rice vinegar

3 tbsp soy sauce

2 tsp soft light brown sugar

2 spring onions (scallions), thinly sliced

1. Preheat the oven to 150°C/130°C fan/300°F/Gas 2. Pat the chicken dry with kitchen paper and season all over. In a bowl, mix the gochujang paste with the honey, soy sauce and sesame oil. Rub half of this all over the chicken, then pop the garlic and ginger inside the cavity.

2. Put the sweet potatoes into a large roasting tray and toss with a little oil and the rest of the honey and gochujang paste, then nestle the chicken into the middle. Roast for 3 hours, basting every so often, until the chicken and sweet potatoes are very tender and sticky.

3. Mix together all the ingredients for the dipping sauce. Carve the chicken and arrange it on a platter with the sweet potatoes. Scatter with the coriander.

4. Serve with the steamed rice and the sharp, spicy sauce for dipping.

SLOW WEEKEND COOKING

French Market Chicken Sunday Lunch

As new parents, we quickly learned that holidays with kids aren't exactly relaxing. It's just more of the same, but with pleasant surroundings and sunshine! The moment you get trapped in a blacked-out hotel room at 7pm with a sleeping child and nowhere to go, it dawns on you that holidays hit differently with children. As a result, Sofie and I build in little escapes throughout the days where one of us will venture out and get some headspace. One such escape resulted in this recipe. One Sunday morning on a family getaway to Auribeau-sur-Siagne, I discovered a little village 700 metres above sea level, Saint-Vallier-de-Thiey. I basked in the silence and read a newspaper (from front to back) with an espresso, then watched the market stalls come to life. Bliss. I returned home with two rotisserie chickens that had been spilling their hot fat on to potatoes beneath since 4am – the makings of the perfect simple lunch.

2 x 1.8kg (4lb) free-range chickens

40g (1½oz) unsalted butter, softened

6 anchovies, finely chopped

2 garlic cloves, crushed

Finely grated zest of 1 lemon

2 tbsp tarragon, finely chopped

120ml (½ cup) white wine

800g (1lb 12oz) baby new potatoes

300g (10oz) fine green beans

Sea salt and freshly ground black pepper

For the dressing

1 tbsp white wine vinegar

Squeeze of lemon juice

2 tsp Dijon mustard

4 tbsp extra virgin olive oil

1 tbsp walnut oil

1. Preheat the oven to 200°C/180°C fan/400°F/Gas 6. Use your fingers to push up from the neck end and gently separate the skin from the breast of the chickens.

2. Mix the butter with the anchovies, garlic, lemon zest and tarragon. Season well and then push this under the skin and spread over the breasts. Put both chickens into a large roasting tin and pour the wine around the outside. Roast for 1 hour until the chickens are golden and the juices run clear when the thickest point of the thigh is pierced with a knife. Leave to rest in a warm place for at least 10 minutes.

3. Meanwhile, cook the baby potatoes in a saucepan of salted boiling water for 15 minutes until tender, then drain. Blanch the beans for 1–2 minutes in boiling water and drain. Toss together in a warm serving bowl.

4. For the dressing, mix the vinegar and lemon juice with the mustard and plenty of seasoning, then gradually whisk in the oils.

5. Pour off the resting juices from the chickens and whisk half into the dressing, then pour this over the beans and potatoes.

6. Carve the chicken and serve with the deliciously dressed potatoes and beans with the remaining resting juices drizzled over the top.

Serves 8

Prep time: 30 minutes

Cook time: 2½ Hours

Tip:

YOU CAN MAKE THE FIRST PART OF THE SAUCE AND SHAPE THE MEATBALLS THE DAY BEFORE, AND KEEP CHILLED IN THE FRIDGE TO FINISH THE NEXT DAY.

Amatriciana Meatballs

It's Saturday evening; the wine is poured, you've gathered friends and family at the table, and you present to them a platter of tender meatballs that have been slowly blipping away in the richest of tomato sauces to coat a big pot of pasta. It's simple, it's homemade and it's perfect. Conversation flows, kids leave the table, the adults keep it going, and right there in that moment, you are creating memories for life. Good times. Don't skimp on the garlic bread, and make sure you add plenty of grated Parmesan from a big block on the table.

600g (1lb 5oz) spaghetti or other long pasta

Extra virgin olive oil, for drizzling

For the sauce

4 x 400g (14oz) tins plum tomatoes

150ml (5fl oz) extra virgin olive oil

2 tbsp unsalted butter

3 garlic cloves, sliced

Pinch of chilli flakes

1 tsp dried oregano

1 onion, halved

30g (1oz) bunch of basil

Sea salt and freshly ground black pepper

For the meatballs

750g (1lb 10oz) minced (ground) beef

120g (4oz) streaky bacon, finely chopped

2 garlic cloves, crushed

50g (2oz) fresh white breadcrumbs

1 medium free-range egg

50g (2oz) Parmesan cheese, finely grated, plus extra to serve

3 tbsp flat-leaf parsley, finely chopped

2 tbsp olive oil, for frying

For the garlic bread

1 large baguette

50g (2oz) salted butter, softened

2 garlic cloves, crushed

3 tbsp flat-leaf parsley, finely chopped

1. Preheat the oven to 160°C/140°C fan/320°F/Gas 3.

2. To make the sauce, crush all the plum tomatoes with your hands or a spoon in a bowl.

3. Heat the oil and butter in a lidded casserole dish over a medium heat. Add the garlic, chilli and oregano, and cook for 5 minutes until lovely and fragrant. Add a third of the crushed tomatoes (put the remaining two-thirds in the fridge for now), followed by the onion and basil, and season with salt and pepper.

4. Bring to a simmer, then transfer to the oven with the lid half on. Cook for 2 hours, stirring every so often until really reduced and thick. Remove the onion and add the rest of the tomatoes, then simmer on the hob over a medium heat for 30 minutes.

5. Meanwhile, make the meatballs. With your hands, combine the minced beef, bacon, crushed garlic, breadcrumbs, egg, Parmesan and half the parsley. Season well and shape into small meatballs.

6. Heat the oil in a large pan and fry the meatballs (in batches if necessary) until golden brown all over, then scoop on to a plate and set aside.

7. Take the baguette and slice part way through at intervals all along the length. Mash the butter with the garlic and parsley, then season and fill the slits in the bread as full as you can with the garlic butter. Wrap in foil and bake in the oven for 10 minutes, then open the top of the foil and cook for 4–5 minutes more to crisp up.

8. Meanwhile, add the browned meatballs to the sauce and simmer gently for 15 minutes until cooked through. At the same time, cook the pasta in a saucepan of boiling salted water for 10 minutes, then drain and drizzle with extra virgin olive oil.

9. Serve the pasta and meatballs topped with a scattering of Parmesan and the remaining parsley with the garlic bread and a green salad on the side.

Serves 6-8 GF

Prep time: 30 minutes

Cook time: 5½ hours,
plus overnight chilling

Tip:

IF YOU HAVE A STANLEY KNIFE, IT WILL MAKE IT EASIER TO GET NICE SCORING ON THE PORK SKIN. YOU WANT THE BLADE TO GO ALL THE WAY THROUGH THE SKIN INTO THE FAT UNDERNEATH. IF YOUR CRACKLING ISN'T AS CRISP AS YOU WOULD LIKE IT AFTER HALF AN HOUR, IT'S BEST TO REMOVE IT ALONG WITH ANY FAT AND POP IT BACK IN WITH THE POTATOES RATHER THAN CONTINUING TO COOK IT ON TOP OF THE PORK, AS YOU DON'T WANT THE MEAT TO DRY OUT.

Slow-roasted Pork Shoulder with Honey & Apple Vinegar Sauce

One of the first family dinners we were able to host once we moved back to Ireland was served up in the dining room of the old Victorian house we were renting. After years of cooking with Californian ingredients, it was exciting and quite grounding to come home to Ireland and rediscover all the great produce this little island has to offer. Fresh seafood, farmhouse cheese, organic vegetables and bloody good meat. The Aga, with which I had a love/hate relationship, was good for one thing, and that was slow-roasting. A stroll to Higgins, our local butcher, resulted in this pork shoulder, which I excitedly served with charred garlic scapes from Drummond House. (Our friends Jeni Glasgow and Reuven Diaz served them as part of the main course at our wedding, and we've been obsessed with them ever since.)

2kg (4lb 8oz) piece of boneless pork shoulder (skin on)

1 tbsp sea salt

1 tbsp fennel seeds

Pinch of chilli flakes (optional)

2 tbsp runny honey

1 tbsp sweet apple cider vinegar

For the Parmesan roasties

1.2kg (2lb 10oz) potatoes, peeled and cut into small chunks

5 tbsp olive oil

40g (1½oz) Parmesan cheese, grated

For the garlicky greens

1 head savoy cabbage, leaves separated

Knob of salted butter

1 tbsp extra virgin olive oil

2 garlic cloves, thinly sliced

Sea salt and freshly ground black pepper

1. Preheat the oven to 150°C/130°C fan/300°F/Gas 2. With a very sharp knife, score the skin of the pork so that it will crackle and crisp.

2. Rub the pork all over with salt and fennel seeds. Put into a roasting tin, pour 300ml (1¼ cups) boiling water around it and cover with foil. Roast in the oven for 5½ hours.

3. At this point, remove the pork from the tin and pour the juices into a jug. Allow the pork to cool and then wrap in foil, leaving the skin exposed, and chill overnight in the fridge.

4. The next day, remove the pork from the fridge an hour before you want to finish cooking it.

5. Put the spuds into a large saucepan of salted water, bring to the boil and simmer for 5 minutes. Drain and return to the pan over a low heat to dry and fluff up the edges.

6. Preheat the oven to 220°C/200°C fan/425°F/Gas 7. Heat the olive oil for the roasties in a tin for a few minutes then add the potatoes and toss well.

7. Put the potatoes in the bottom of the oven and return the pork to the top to crisp the crackling (see Tip). Cook both for 30 minutes, then remove the pork and set aside, covered in foil. Turn the spuds and cook for a further 15 minutes, then generously sprinkle with the Parmesan and cook for 10 minutes more until the cheese is golden.

8. Meanwhile, discard any fat from the juices in your jug and pour the juices into a saucepan over a medium heat. Add the honey and vinegar and bubble together.

9. Put the whole leaves of cabbage into a pan, add a splash of water, then cover and steam for 2–3 minutes. Uncover and add the butter, olive oil and garlic, and cook for 1 minute more. Season to taste.

10. Slice the pork and crackling and serve with the juices, golden crispy Parmesan potatoes and garlicky cabbage.

Little Food Wins & Flavour-Makers

1. Grilled Sticky Pomegranate Chicken with Red Onion & Coriander Salad
2. Harissa Fried Chicken with Garlic & Herb Aioli
3. Bang Bang Poached Chicken Salad with Lime, Coriander & Mint
4. Nam Jim Sticky Pork with Clanky Herb Salad
5. Peanut Butter Pork Mince Satay Noodles
6. Autumn Pasta with Blue Cheese & Nuts
7. Instant Ramen Upgrade
8. Gnocci with Soy Butter Sauce, Broccoli & Sesame
9. Cheat's Hummus Salad Bowl
10. Soy-Brined Blackened Cod with Greens & Rice
11. Fennel & Orange Rubbed Pork Chops with Brown Spring Onions & Salad Leaves
12. Chilli Oil Late Night Noodles
13. Sichuan Numbing Cauliflower "Wings"
14. Korean-Cut Beef Short Ribs with Banchan & Rice
15. Crispy Spice Bag Chicken Buns
16. Prawn & Dill Rolls with Wild Garlic Mayo

Grilled Sticky Pomegranate Chicken with Red Onion & Coriander Salad

This recipe can easily be cooked on the stovetop, but it also works particularly well once a little smoke and flame hits the chicken skin. I would suggest you grill the seasoned chicken thighs over the flame until all but cooked and then finish them in the pan of sticky red sauce to make them deliciously addictive. Served up with red onion, coriander and ruby jewels of pomegranate, you will be left with a dish sure to brighten up even the darkest winter day.

2 tbsp olive oil

8 free-range chicken thighs (bone in and skin on)

6 spring onions (scallions), thinly sliced

2 garlic cloves, thinly sliced

3cm (1¼in) piece of fresh ginger, grated

2 tsp ras el hanout

3 tbsp pomegranate molasses

200ml (generous ¾ cup) chicken stock

3 tbsp soft light brown sugar

Large handful of flat-leaf parsley, roughly chopped

Sea salt and freshly ground black pepper

Cooked bulgur wheat, to serve

For the red onion and coriander salad

2 red onions, thinly sliced

Juice of 1 lemon

1 tbsp sesame oil

Seeds of 1 pomegranate

Large bunch of coriander (cilantro), leaves picked

1. Heat the oil in a large frying pan (skillet) over a medium–high heat. Season the chicken and brown all over until the skin is golden, about 5–6 minutes. Remove and set aside.

2. Add the spring onions, garlic, ginger and ras el hanout to the pan and fry for a couple of minutes, then add the pomegranate molasses, stock and sugar. Once bubbling, return the chicken to the pan and bubble over a medium heat for 15 minutes until the chicken is cooked through.

3. Meanwhile, put the red onion into a bowl and squeeze over the lemon juice. Season well, then add the sesame oil and pomegranate seeds and leave to macerate.

4. Once the chicken is cooked, scatter with the parsley. Toss the coriander leaves through the onion and pomegranate salad and serve the chicken and salad with cooked bulgur wheat.

Serves 6–8

Prep time: 15 minutes,
plus marinating

Cook time: 45 minutes

Harissa Fried Chicken with Garlic & Herb Aioli

This addictive crispy chicken, fuzzy with harissa spice, is a next-level dinner! Serve it with a lightly dressed crisp green salad or with crispy new potatoes. Any leftover aioli will keep in the fridge for 10 days.

200g (7oz) Greek yoghurt

2 tbsp rose harissa paste

3 garlic cloves, grated

50ml (scant ¼ cup) white wine vinegar or distilled malt vinegar

8 skinless chicken thigh fillets, sliced into strips

1 litre (4 cups) vegetable oil, for frying

Sea salt and freshly ground black pepper

For the coating

180g (1½ cups) plain (all-purpose) flour

60g (2¼oz) cornflour (cornstarch)

1 tsp ground cumin

½ tsp ground coriander

1 tsp sweet smoked paprika

For the aioli

2 large handfuls of mixed picked coriander (cilantro), mint and parsley leaves

2 garlic cloves, crushed

2 tsp white wine vinegar

2 medium free-range egg yolks

175ml (¾ cup) vegetable oil

100ml (scant ½ cup) light olive oil

1. Mix the yoghurt, harissa paste, garlic and vinegar together and season well with salt and pepper. Add the chicken strips and set aside in the fridge to marinate for at least 1 hour, or overnight.

2. To make the aioli, put the herbs, garlic, vinegar and egg yolks into a food processor and blitz together. Gradually, with the motor running, drizzle in the oils until you have a smooth, thick aioli (you may not need all the oil). Scoop into a bowl for serving.

3. In a shallow dish, mix together the dry ingredients for the coating and season with salt and pepper.

4. Heat the 1 litre (4 cups) oil in a deep frying pan (skillet) over a medium heat until it reaches 180°C/350°F, or until a cube of bread turns golden brown in 30 seconds.

5. Remove the chicken from the marinade, shaking off any excess, and coat all over in the flour mix. Dip back into the marinade and then once more into the flour mix. Working in batches, fry the coated chicken in the hot oil for 5 minutes until golden and crisp. Drain on a plate lined with kitchen paper.

6. Once all the chicken is fried, serve with the bright green herb aioli.

Serves 4–6   DF

Prep time: 15 minutes,
plus cooling

Cook time: 1 hour

Bang Bang Poached Chicken Salad with Lime, Coriander & Mint

This is my riff on those 'Chinese-style' American salads that seem to be standard fare wherever you travel in the States. Although perhaps a little uncool, they make a tasty little summer supper, and the dressing alone is something I revisit on the regular.

1 small free-range chicken

500ml (2 cups) fresh chicken stock

2 star anise

2 tsp Sichuan peppercorns

3cm (1¼in) piece of fresh ginger, peeled and cut into strips

1 large cucumber, peeled, cored and cut into bite-sized chunks

2 large carrots, julienned

⅓ red cabbage, finely shredded

Large handful of coriander (cilantro), leaves torn

40g (1½oz) roasted peanuts, chopped

For the dressing

4 tbsp crunchy peanut butter

1 tbsp maple syrup

5 tbsp soy sauce

4 tbsp rice vinegar

1 long red chilli, thinly sliced

½ tsp ground Sichuan peppercorns

2 tbsp toasted sesame oil

1. Put the chicken into a deep saucepan and pour over the stock, along with enough water to just cover the chicken. Add the spices and ginger and bring to the boil, then reduce the heat to a simmer and cook very gently for 45 minutes. Allow to cool in the liquid until you can handle it easily (keep the liquid for the next steps).

2. Mix together all the dressing ingredients with 4 tablespoons of the cooking liquid and set aside.

3. Once the chicken is cool enough to handle, shred the meat from the bones and mix with 100ml (scant ½ cup) of the cooking liquid.

4. Bash the cucumber lightly with a rolling pin, then toss with the carrots and cabbage in a serving bowl. Add the chicken, coriander leaves and dressing and lightly toss. Serve scattered with peanuts.

Serves 4–6   DF GF

Prep time: 20 minutes

Cook time: 5–6 minutes

Tip:

IF USING WOODEN SKEWERS, SOAK THEM IN COLD WATER FOR ABOUT HALF AN HOUR BEFORE USING TO PREVENT THEM BURNING.

Nam Jim Sticky Pork with Clanky Herb Salad

These sticky pork skewers are ideally cooked over hot coals, but you can also use a griddle pan to give those lovely deep char marks and smoky flavour. Serve with steamed rice to make a more generous meal. The *nam jim* dressing is a must; there's very little that doesn't benefit from that smack of sweet, sour, savoury and hot liquid.

2 pork fillets (about 900g/2lb), cut into long, thin strips

1 tbsp oyster sauce

1 tsp groundnut (peanut) oil

For the *nam jim* dressing

3 tbsp palm or soft dark brown sugar

5 tbsp fish sauce

2 garlic cloves, grated

2 spring onions (scallions), thinly sliced

1 red chilli, finely chopped

Juice of 3 limes

For the salad

1 Chinese leaf cabbage, cut into thin wedges

1 cucumber, peeled, cored and chopped

200g (7oz) radishes, halved or quartered

150g (5oz) mangetout, halved lengthways

2 handfuls of pea shoots

Handful of coriander (cilantro) leaves

Small handful of mint leaves

2–3 sprigs of Thai basil, leaves stripped

2 tbsp sesame seeds, toasted

2 tbsp toasted sesame oil

1. Put the pork strips into a shallow dish. Mix together all the ingredients for the *nam jim* and pour a third of this dressing over the pork. Add the oyster sauce and groundnut oil and mix well. Put the rest of the dressing into a separate bowl for the next step.

2. To prepare the salad, toss together all the veggies, herbs and sesame seeds. Mix the sesame oil with the rest of the *nam jim* dressing, then pour over the salad and toss to coat.

3. Thread the pork onto wooden or metal skewers. Place a heavy-based frying pan (skillet) or griddle (grill) pan over a high heat. When hot, add the pork skewers and fry for 5–6 minutes, turning once or twice, until sticky and just cooked. Serve the skewers with the salad.

Peanut Butter Pork Mince Satay Noodles

My go-to Friday night quick-fix dinner. If you have the key ingredients for this dish stocked in your kitchen, you'll find it's one that comes together quickly and with little fuss. The payoff is a rich peanut butter satay sauce that's the perfect combination of salty, sour and sweet, slathered over rice noodles with plenty of crunchy veggies.

300g (10oz) flat rice noodles

2 tbsp groundnut (peanut) or vegetable oil

2 garlic cloves, sliced

3cm (1¼in) piece of fresh ginger, peeled and cut into thin matchsticks

1 long red chilli, thinly sliced

Bunch of spring onions (scallions), roughly chopped

500g (1lb 2oz) minced (ground) pork

200g (7oz) sugar snap peas

150g (5oz) pak choi, sliced

Large handful of coriander (cilantro) leaves

Small handful of peanuts, roughly chopped

For the dressing

4 tbsp sesame oil

2 tbsp soy sauce

2 tbsp fish sauce

2 tbsp crunchy peanut butter

Juice of 2 limes

2 tbsp soft light brown sugar

1. Bring a pan of water to the boil and cook the noodles for 2–3 minutes, then drain and rinse in warm water to stop them sticking together. Tip into a bowl and set aside.

2. Heat the oil in a frying pan (skillet) over a medium heat and fry the garlic, ginger, chilli and most of the spring onions for 5 minutes. Add the minced pork, increase the heat and cook until browned all over.

3. While the mince is browning, mix together all the ingredients for the dressing in a bowl.

4. Add the sugar snaps, pak choi and a small splash of water to the pan and cook for 1–2 minutes. Pour over the dressing and leave to bubble for 30 seconds before adding the noodles. If your noodles look slightly dry, don't be afraid to add another splash of water. Scatter over the coriander, toss together and serve with a sprinkle of chopped peanuts and the remaining spring onions.

Serves 4   V

Prep time: 15 minutes

Cook time: 45 minutes

Autumn Pasta with Blue Cheese & Nuts

I love the sticky sound this steamy pasta makes as you stir through pumpkin, walnuts and blue cheese until it forms a creamy sauce. It's proper autumnal food – seek out smaller, sweeter pumpkins with interesting textures and skin colours; they are far more flavourful than the regular large orange ones. I particularly love the pastel blue-green-skinned Crown Prince variety grown by McNally's Family Farm in North County Dublin – a visit to their farm shop in autumn always provides plenty of dinner inspiration.

1 pumpkin or autumn squash (about 1kg/2lb 4oz), peeled, deseeded and sliced

3–4 sprigs of thyme

1 tbsp olive oil

1 tbsp salted butter

2 onions, thinly sliced

350g (12oz) pasta shapes, such as conchiglie or rigatoni

100g (3½oz) blue cheese

75g (3oz) walnuts, toasted and roughly crushed

Sea salt and freshly ground black pepper

Best-quality extra virgin olive oil, to serve

1. Preheat the oven to 200°C/180°C fan/400°F/Gas 6.

2. Place the pumpkin on a large baking sheet with the thyme sprigs and toss in the olive oil until all the pieces are coated. Season generously with salt and pepper. Roast in the oven for 40 minutes, or until tender and caramelised at the edges. Once cooked, keep warm.

3. While the pumpkin cooks, place a large heavy-based frying pan (skillet) over a medium–high heat and add the butter. Add the onions and season generously, tossing to coat completely in the melted butter. Reduce the heat and cook gently until the onions are sweet and caramelised, about 10–15 minutes.

4. Towards the end of the pumpkin cooking time, bring a large pan of water to the boil and generously season with salt. Once boiling, add the pasta and cook until al dente. Drain and reserve a cup of the starchy cooking water for use in the sauce.

5. Increase the heat back up under the pan with the onions, then add the reserved pasta water and bring to a steady simmer. Meanwhile, mash half the cooked pumpkin and add this to the onions. Crumble in almost all of the blue cheese (keep a little back to serve) and stir until you have a smooth, creamy sauce. Working quickly, add the pasta to the pan and stir through until completely coated.

6. Serve the pasta hot in warmed plates topped with the remaining pumpkin slices and blue cheese. Sprinkle with toasted crushed walnuts and top with a generous drizzle of the best-quality extra virgin olive oil you have to hand and a last seasoning of sea salt and black pepper.

LITTLE FOOD WINS & FLAVOUR-MAKERS

Serves 1   V DF

Prep time: 10 minutes, plus
marinating

Cook time: 5 minutes

Tip:

TAKE THIS TO THE NEXT LEVEL BY ADDING SOME SHREDDED
ROAST CHICKEN OR PORK, OR SOME CRISPY FRIED CUBES OF
TOFU – OR GO THE OTHER WAY AND LEAVE OUT THE EGG TO
MAKE THIS VEGAN. YOU CAN MAKE A BATCH OF THE MARINATED
EGGS AND KEEP THEM (IN THEIR SHELLS IN THE MARINADE)
IN THE FRIDGE FOR UP TO A WEEK.

TOGARASHI SEASONING IS A BLEND OF CHILLI, SEAWEED AND
SESAME SEEDS, AND ADDS A GREAT HIT OF FLAVOUR WITHOUT
HAVING TO GET THEM ALL SEPARATELY. IF YOU CAN'T GET IT,
THEN USE TOASTED SESAME SEEDS AND A PINCH OF CHILLI FLAKES.

Instant Ramen Upgrade

While hosting *Saturday Kitchen* on BBC One, I had the unique opportunity to meet some incredible chefs and food writers. Over the course of the rehearsals the day before and the morning of the show, there was plenty of time to get to know them. One of my favourite guest chefs was Tim Anderson, *MasterChef* winner and food writer ,who has written five cookbooks on Japanese cuisine. He made a version of this instant noodle upgrade, and I've been making it ever since. It takes one of those cheap packets of noodles and makes it worthy of dinnertime, without making you feel like you've completely fallen back into student-style eating.

1 free-range egg

2 tbsp soy sauce

1 tbsp mirin

10g (¼oz) dried mushrooms

2 tsp vegetable oil

1 tbsp sesame oil

1 garlic clove, thinly sliced

50g (2oz) shredded greens, such as kale or cavolo nero

1 x pack or pot instant ramen noodles (your favourite flavour)

2 tsp miso paste

2 spring onions (scallions), thinly sliced

Togarashi seasoning

Japanese pickles or kimchi, to serve

1. Put the egg into a pan of cold water, then bring to the boil and cook for 6 minutes. Cool under cold running water, then tap lightly all over to crack the shell a little.

2. Mix together the soy sauce and mirin in a bowl and add the egg, still in its shell. Leave to marinate for at least an hour or two (overnight is best) then peel; you will see it has a lovely marbled pattern. Reserve the marinade.

3. Pour boiling water over the dried mushrooms until they are just covered (about 120ml/½ cup) and leave to soak for 10 minutes.

4. Heat the vegetable oil and half the sesame oil in a frying pan (skillet) over a medium heat. Add the garlic and greens and stir-fry until fragrant, then add a splash of water, cover and steam until tender.

5. Prepare the noodles according to the packet instructions, adding the miso paste as well as the flavour sachet from the packet. Strain the mushrooms, reserving the liquid (discard any gritty bits), and add half the mushroom soaking liquid (discard the rest) to the noodles.

6. Transfer the noodles into a bowl and top with the mushrooms and greens, along with the remaining sesame oil, some togarashi seasoning and the egg, halved. Drizzle some of the soy and mirin marinade over the top and serve with Japanese pickles or kimchi.

Gnocchi with Soy Butter Sauce, Broccoli & Sesame

My love affair with shop-bought gnocchi as a cheat's kitchen pantry staple continues unabated. One of my most popular recipes is a salty, creamy pasta with soy sauce and butter, which led me to this. It works beautifully with gnocchi and you can have it on the table in less than 30 minutes.

60g (2¼oz) salted butter

2 tbsp sesame oil, plus extra for drizzling

Pinch of chilli flakes

3 garlic cloves, thinly sliced

3 tbsp soy sauce

250g (9oz) Tenderstem broccoli or calabrese florets

400g (14oz) fresh gnocchi

1 tbsp sesame seeds, toasted

Large handful of basil leaves

1. Place a frying pan (skillet) over a medium–high heat and add the butter and sesame oil. Once the butter starts to foam, add the chilli flakes and garlic and cook for 1 minute, then add the soy sauce.

2. Meanwhile, cook the broccoli in a large pan of boiling water for 3 minutes. Remove with a slotted spoon and drain well.

3. Return the water to the boil, season with a little salt and add the gnocchi. Cook until they float to the surface, then remove with a slotted spoon straight into the pan of sauce, along with the broccoli.

4. Toss well and serve with a drizzle of sesame oil and scattered with sesame seeds and basil leaves.

Serves 4 V

Prep time: 15 minutes

Cook time: 5 minutes

Tip:

IF YOU HAVE MORE TIME, ROAST THE CHICKPEAS IN A HOT OVEN WITH A DRIZZLE OF OLIVE OIL AND SALT AND PEPPER FOR 15 MINUTES UNTIL THEY ARE GOLDEN AND A BIT CRISPY.

Cheat's Hummus Salad Bowl

I have a long-standing failed ambition to recover the brief moment in my late teens when I had something that resembled a six pack. These flurries of good intentional eating are now summed up by what I refer to as my 'Dad Bod' diet. They last about a week or two, during which time I meal-prep wildly, packing the fridge with healthy ingredients that can be assembled easily in a bowl and eaten with a virtuous smug grin. This recipe is an ode to the DB; when you do need those moments of lighter eating, use it as a base for assembling somewhat healthy dishes.

200g (7oz) good-quality hummus

Finely grated zest and juice of 1 lemon

1 garlic clove, grated

3 tbsp extra virgin olive oil

1 red onion, thinly sliced

400g (14oz) tin chickpeas, drained and rinsed

2 romaine lettuces, leaves roughly torn

1 radicchio (or 2 red chicories), leaves separated

½ large cucumber, halved lengthways and sliced

125g (4oz) cherry tomatoes, halved

Dusting of sumac

Sea salt and freshly ground black pepper

For the za'atar croutons

3 slices of sourdough bread (about 100g/3½oz)

3 tbsp olive oil

1 tsp za'atar

For the dressing

75g (3oz) natural yoghurt

1 garlic clove, grated

Squeeze of lemon juice

3 tbsp extra virgin olive oil

Small splash of water, to loosen

1. Start with the croutons: tear the bread into bite-sized pieces. Heat the oil in a frying pan (skillet) over a medium heat and fry the bread until golden. Drain on kitchen paper and sprinkle with za'atar and sea salt. Set aside.

2. Mix together all the ingredients for the dressing and season to taste.

3. Whip the hummus with the lemon zest, garlic and 1 tablespoon of the extra virgin olive oil.

4. Squeeze the lemon juice over the sliced red onion, season with sea salt and add the rest of the extra virgin olive oil. Set aside.

5. Warm the chickpeas in the crouton pan for a few minutes.

6. Arrange the salad leaves, cucumber and cherry tomatoes in a large serving bowl. Scatter with the red onion and warmed chickpeas, then toss with the dressing. Spoon the hummus on to the salad and dust with sumac, then finish with the za'atar croutons.

Prep time: 10 minutes,
plus marinating

Cook time: 10 minutes

Soy-Brined Blackened Cod with Greens & Rice

When I lived in Los Angeles, I was asked to appear in one of those infomercials you see for products that promise to change your life. I have always had an aversion to stupid kitchen gadgets; my advice would be to just invest in timeless items like heavy-duty pans, good chopping boards and proper knives. But in the land of bright lights and people promising to make you a star, things were different. The product I was sent was a multicooker. To be fair, it was pretty damn good, so I agreed. I arrived on set, met my co-star and got to work. We braised meat, 'baked' bread and even made yoghurt; this thing was just short of solving world peace by the end of the day. I had to hide my smirk as I uttered the words: 'You just set it and forget it!' Seven years later and a transatlantic move home, and the aforementioned multicooker is still going strong. We use it primarily to cook rice and grains, which it does exceptionally well, and when you've got good rice, a dish like this, with fresh fish and simple greens, is a cinch to pull together.

4 x 200g (7oz) cod loin fillets

6 tbsp soy sauce

2 tbsp rice vinegar

1 tbsp sesame oil, plus extra for drizzling

250g (9oz) basmati rice

75ml (⅓ cup) mirin

75ml (⅓ cup) sake

2 tbsp miso paste

1 tbsp caster (superfine) sugar

300g (10oz) Asian greens (pak choi, tat soi, choi sum), sliced

1 tbsp black and white sesame seeds, toasted

1. Put the cod fillets into a dish and add the soy sauce, rice vinegar and sesame oil. Leave to marinate for 30 minutes to an hour, turning every so often.

2. Rinse the rice, then add to a saucepan and cover with 400ml (1¾ cups) cold water. Season and bring to the boil, then cover with a lid and simmer for 8 minutes. Turn off the heat and leave to steam, then fluff up with a fork.

3. Meanwhile, in a bowl, mix together the mirin, sake, miso paste and caster sugar.

4. Steam the greens for 1–2 minutes until just tender.

5. Heat a non-stick frying pan (skillet) over a medium–high heat. Remove the cod from the brine and add half the brine to the mirin mixture.

6. Drizzle the cod with a little extra sesame oil and add to the pan (cook in batches if necessary). Cook for 3–4 minutes until nice and caramelised on the bottom. Remove from the pan and set aside on a plate.

7. Add the mirin blend to the pan and bubble away until it starts to thicken. Return the fish to the pan, blackened-side down, and cook for a further 2 minutes, then flip over and cook for 1–2 minutes more until the fish is just cooked and the sauce is thick and sticky and coating the fish.

8. Serve the blackened, sticky fish on a bed of rice and greens, scattered with toasted sesame seeds.

Serves 4   DF GF

Prep time: 10 minutes

Cook time: 15 minutes

Tip:

USE A MANDOLINE, IF YOU HAVE ONE, TO CUT THE FENNEL INTO VERY THIN SLICES: A GOOD SHARP KNIFE WILL DO IF NOT.

Fennel & Orange Rubbed Pork Chops with Browned Spring Onions & Salad Leaves

One of the saving graces of arriving home to Ireland in the midst of the first Covid lockdown was our proximity to Higgins Butchers in Sutton. Masked up, this is where I had those few social interactions with the outside world, and I got to choose most of our dinners from the impressive display of meat on the butcher counter. Rick does proper pork chops; these beauties were bone in and skin on, and full of flavour.

When cooking chops in a pan, I highly recommend you use tongs to hold them skin-side down in the pan, pressing until the fat renders and you end up with irresistible crisp, golden edges. I particularly love these pork chops dusted in ground fennel seeds, orange zest and plenty of sea salt, which will become aromatic in the hot pork fat.

4 (or 2, if very large) outdoor-reared pork chops, skin and fat on

2 large oranges

1 tbsp fennel seeds

2 tbsp olive oil

2 bunches of spring onions (scallions), trimmed but left whole

2 garlic cloves, bashed

1 large fennel bulb, very thinly sliced (use a mandoline here if possible)

4 sprigs of dill, fronds picked

Handful of flat-leaf parsley, leaves picked

2 baby gem lettuces, leaves separated

Sea salt and freshly ground black pepper

For the dressing

Juice of 1 lemon

Juice of ½ orange

Good pinch of chilli flakes

1 tsp runny honey

2 tbsp extra virgin olive oil

1. Preheat the oven to 190°C/170°C fan/375°F/Gas 5.

2. Take the pork chops and use a pair of scissors to snip into the fat to create a hedgehog effect. Transfer to a dish and finely grate over the orange zest, then add the fennel seeds and half the olive oil. Season well and use your hands to rub the flavours into the pork.

3. Heat the rest of the olive oil in an ovenproof heavy-based frying pan (skillet) over a medium heat. Add the

spring onions and cook until browned and softened. Set aside.

4. Add the pork chops to the pan and brown well on both sides, then use kitchen tongs to stand them on their ends to help cook the fat and skin. Add the garlic to the pan and a small splash of water, then transfer to the oven to finish cooking through for 8–10 minutes, depending on thickness. Set aside to rest on a warm plate covered with foil while you prepare the salad.

5. Peel and segment the oranges. Toss the segments with the very finely shaved fennel, along with the herbs, baby gem leaves and charred spring onions.

6. To make the dressing, mix the lemon and orange juices with the chilli flakes, honey and plenty of seasoning. Whisk in the oil and 3 tablespoons of the resting juices from the pork before tossing into the salad. Serve the pork chops with the dressed salad alongside.

Serves 2   V DF

Prep time: 5 minutes

Cook time: 10 minutes

Chilli Oil Late Night Noodles

On Tuesday nights in Highland Park, the neighbourhood next to our home in Eagle Rock, California, the streets come alive with street-food vendors. I first went down there to check out the vegan tacos, which were particularly good and a regular favourite for dinner, even as a non-vegan! As more vendors joined the party, it was hard not to be impressed and distracted by the hand-pulled noodles being made at the roadside. That particular stall always had a long queue, and the smells of chilli oil and Sichuan peppercorns were pretty irresistible as they hit the freshly cooked noodles. I don't have the time, patience or skills to make my own noodles midweek at home, but this dish takes inspiration from those warm evenings on the streets of Highland Park.

2 fat garlic cloves, crushed with 1 tsp flaky sea salt

1 long red chilli, thinly sliced

1 tsp Sichuan peppercorns, lightly bashed in a pestle and mortar

2 tbsp Chinese black rice vinegar (or rice vinegar)

4 tbsp soy sauce

Good pinch of caster (superfine) sugar

4 spring onions (scallions), thinly sliced, white and green parts separated

500g g (10oz) fat fresh or frozen udon noodles

3 tbsp groundnut (peanut) oil

1 tbsp sesame seeds, toasted

1. Put the garlic, chilli, Sichuan peppercorns, vinegar, soy sauce, sugar and the white parts of the spring onions into a bowl.

2. Cook the noodles in boiling water until piping hot (about 8–10 minutes, but check the packet), then drain and run under warm water to stop them sticking.

3. Heat the oil in a small pan over a high heat until really hot and sizzling, then pour this over the bowl of aromatics, quickly followed by the noodles. Toss well and divide between two bowls. Top with the sliced green spring onions and the sesame seeds and serve.

Serves 4–6   V DF GF

Prep time: 20 minutes

Cook time: 40 minutes

Sichuan Numbing Cauliflower Wings

On our first trip to San Francisco, Sofie and I made a beeline for the much-hyped Mission Chinese by chef Danny Bowien. It was probably the first time we'd experienced long lines outside the doors of restaurants, such were the excitement levels with new hot spots to eat. Mission Chinese became a hit for its creative mash-ups and takes on classic Chinese restaurant food. Dishes like thrice-cooked bacon with bitter melon and sizzling cumin lamb belly wowed, but the insanely popular Chongqing chicken wings were unforgettable for their lip-tingling quantity of Sichuan peppercorns. The spice mix here works a treat on chicken wings, but this vegan alternative for cauliflower 'wings' is pretty addictive.

For the 'wings'

2 large cauliflowers, cut into medium florets

1 tbsp cornflour (cornstarch)

1 tbsp semolina

½ tsp baking powder

4 tbsp vegetable oil

4 spring onions (scallions), thinly sliced

1 long red chilli, thinly sliced

Sea salt and freshly ground white pepper

For the numbing spice blend

½ tbsp Sichuan peppercorns

½ tbsp cumin seeds

1 tsp fennel seeds

1 tsp red chilli flakes

1 star anise

1 tsp flaky sea salt

1 tbsp soft dark brown sugar

1. Preheat the oven to 200°C/180°C fan/400°F/Gas 6.

2. Toss the cauliflower, cornflour, semolina and baking powder together in a large bowl. Season well and spread out on a baking sheet, then drizzle with 3 tablespoons of the oil. Roast for 40 minutes until golden and crispy, turning once halfway through cooking.

3. Meanwhile, set a dry frying pan (skillet) over a low heat and toast the whole spices until fragrant. Transfer to a pestle and mortar and bash until coarsely ground, then mix with the salt and sugar.

4. Heat the remaining oil in a small frying pan over a medium–high heat. Add the spring onions and chilli and fry until translucent and crisp. Drain on kitchen paper.

5. Once the cauliflower is golden and crispy, toss with the spice blend, then scatter over the chilli and spring onions and serve immediately.

Serves 6   DF

Prep time: 30 minutes, plus marinating and resting

Cook time: 5 minutes

Korean-Cut Beef Short Ribs with *Banchan* & Rice

Tip:

DON'T WORRY IF YOU CAN'T GET THE SUPER-THIN FLANKEN-CUT SHORT RIBS: YOU CAN USE BAVETTE OR ONGLET OR THICKER CUT SHORT RIBS INSTEAD. JUST COOK IT FOR A COUPLE OF EXTRA MINUTES AS IT IS A LITTLE THICKER AND YOU CAN USE SCISSORS TO SNIP IT INTO SMALLER PIECES. SSAMJANG IS A SWEET AND SPICY KOREAN CONDIMENT THAT YOU'LL FIND IN ASIAN SUPERMARKETS OR ONLINE – IT KEEPS IN THE FRIDGE FOR MONTHS. FINALLY, A NASHI IS A CRISP, ALMOST APPLE-LIKE PEAR WITH A TANGY FLAVOUR. YOU CAN SOMETIMES SPOT IT IN ASIAN GROCERY STORES, BUT ANY NOT-QUITE-RIPE PEAR WILL WORK.

My knowledge of Korean cuisine is somewhat limited to a single visit to Seoul for a TV show and a love of eating in Korean restaurants. However, these Korean-style short ribs have become a bit of a regular feast for the family, after our friends DJ and Grace made them for us one evening. It's the kind of supper that is even more delicious cooked over a hot grill. Much of the *banchan* (side dishes that accompany the main event) can be shop-bought or prepared in advance.

800g (1lb 12oz) short ribs cut flanken-style (see Tip)

75ml (⅓ cup) soy sauce

75ml (⅓ cup) rice wine or sake (or use water)

3 tbsp runny honey

1 small onion

1 small firm pear (nashi, if you can find it), peeled and cored

5 garlic cloves

Thumb-sized piece of fresh ginger, grated

2 tbsp sesame oil

2 tsp ground black pepper

1 tbsp gochujang paste

For the pickled cucumbers

6 baby cucumbers (or 1 large)

1 tbsp flaky sea salt

2 tbsp rice vinegar

1 tbsp sesame oil

1 tbsp sesame seeds, toasted

1 garlic clove, crushed

2 tsp soft dark brown sugar

2 tsp fish sauce

2 tsp gochujang paste

To serve

1 tbsp sesame seeds, toasted

2 spring onions (scallions), thinly sliced

Steamed rice

Kimchi

Korean or Japanese pickles

Little gem lettuce leaves, separated

Ssamjang

1. Put the ribs into a container. Mix the soy sauce with the rice wine or water and honey and pour over the ribs. In a small food processor, blitz the onion, pear, garlic, and grated ginger to a smooth paste and add this to the ribs, along with the sesame oil, pepper and gochujang. Turn to coat evenly and mix, then leave to marinate for at least 2 hours.

2. To make the pickled cucumber, slice the cucumbers into rounds, sprinkle with salt and leave to drain in a sieve over a bowl while you mix together the rest of the pickle ingredients. Rinse the cucumbers and pat them dry, then toss in the pickling mixture and leave for at least an hour.

3. When you are ready to cook the ribs, remove them from the marinade, shaking off any excess (discard the marinade). Place the ribs on a barbecue over direct heat or in a griddle pan set over a high heat and cook for 2 minutes on each side (or 4–5 minutes if you have a thicker cut), or until you have deep char marks on the outside and the beef is still slightly pink inside (medium-rare).

4. Rest the ribs for 5 minutes, covered with foil, then slice into bite-sized pieces.

5. To serve, arrange the meat on a warmed platter, scattered with toasted sesame seeds and spring onions. Bring to the table with bowls of rice, the pickled cucumber, kimchi, pickles, lettuce leaves and the *ssamjang* sauce.

Serves 4   DF

Prep time: 15 minutes

Cook time: 30 minutes

Tip:

YOU COULD, I SUPPOSE, COOK THIS IN AN AIR FRYER. I WON'T JUDGE YOU (MAYBE JUST A LITTLE), BUT I WOULD ENCOURAGE YOU TO TRY THE DEEP-FRIED VERSION BEFORE YOU DO.

Crispy Spice Bag Chicken Buns

Fried chicken was most definitely having a moment while we were living in Los Angeles. (Although, when is it not having a moment?) Howlin' Ray's was THE place while we lived there and – no joke – people would line up around the block in Chinatown to get their hands on a paper-wrapped Nashville-style chicken bun doused in fiery red spice. Now for the Irish mash-up. Outside Ireland, most people won't have a clue what a spice bag is, but those in the know will be well aware that this Chinese-Irish takeaway staple is fast becoming a favourite. Crisp, fried chicken tossed in a sweet spice mixture with chips and fried onions and peppers, all served in a paper bag and devoured – typically after a night out. I want all of that, but I want it in an LA-style bun – hook it to my veins!

1 litre (4 cups) vegetable oil, for frying

2 tsp chilli flakes

3 garlic cloves, thinly sliced

1 red chilli, thinly sliced

6 spring onions (scallions), thinly sliced diagonally

8 skinless chicken thigh fillets, cut into strips

4 tbsp cornflour (cornstarch)

2 tbsp plain (all-purpose) flour

Generous pinch of salt and ground white pepper

1 tbsp sesame oil

1–2 tbsp Shaoxing wine (or use rice wine)

4 brioche buns

1 gem or ½ iceberg lettuce, shredded

For the spice mix

1 tbsp Chinese five-spice

½ tsp garlic powder

1 tsp chilli powder

⅛ tsp each of ground cardamom, cinnamon and ginger

2 tsp salt

2 tsp granulated sugar

½ tsp white pepper

For the mayo

4–5 tbsp good-quality mayonnaise

1 tbsp sriracha sauce

1. Mix together all the ingredients for the spice mix and set aside.

2. Place a large frying pan (skillet) over a high heat; once smoking, add 2 tablespoons of the vegetable oil. When the oil is hot, add the chilli flakes, garlic, red chilli and spring onions and stir-fry for 3–5 minutes until the chilli and spring onion are tender and translucent, then remove from the heat.

3. In a bowl, combine the chicken with 1 tablespoon of the spice mix, along with the cornflour, plain flour, salt, white pepper and sesame oil. Add 4–5 tablespoons of water to loosen the mix and coat the chicken all over.

4. Pour the remaining oil into a deep wok or heavy-based saucepan over a medium heat and heat to 180°C/350°F (you'll know when it's ready when a cube of bread browns in 45 seconds). Fry the chicken in batches for 6–8 minutes, or until crisp and golden. Drain on a plate lined with kitchen paper.

5. Return the pan with the chilli and spring onion to the heat. Add the cooked chicken, then pour in the Shaoxing wine and stir-fry until the chicken is warmed through.

6. Meanwhile, lightly toast the brioche buns and mix the mayonnaise with the sriracha.

7. Sprinkle the remaining spice mix over the chicken and toss well. Spread the mayo over the base of the buns, top with shredded lettuce, then the chicken and top with the bun lids.

Make-Ahead Plates For Feasts

Here are some easy plates you can make ahead of time for events and large gatherings with friends and family. You can tweak the recipes as you like and the photos aren't of the actual recipes here – simply some plates I've loved making recently. I hope they give you some idea of what you can throw together!

Summer Tomato Platter with Toasted Fennel Seeds

Slice 800g (1lb 12oz) mixed heirloom tomatoes and arrange on a platter. Toast 2 teaspoons of green fennel seeds in a pan and roughly crush them in a pestle and mortar, then whisk with 2 teaspoons of sweet apple cider vinegar and some sea salt and black pepper. Mix in 3 tablespoons of extra virgin olive oil and pour over the tomatoes. Add plenty of basil and Parmesan shavings, and serve with crusty bread to mop up the juices.

Cucumber Platter

Peel, deseed and chop 2 large cucumbers into small pieces and put into a serving dish. Scatter with black olives, crumbled feta cheese and very thinly sliced red onion. Make a dressing: mix together the juice of a lemon, a pinch of chilli flakes, the leaves from 3 sprigs of fresh oregano, a drizzle of honey and plenty of seasoning, then whisk in 3–4 tablespoons of extra virgin olive oil. Pour over the cucumber and serve.

Chickpea Salad with Red Onion, Parsley & Toasted Cumin

Drain and rinse 2 x 400g (14oz) tins of chickpeas and tumble into a serving dish. Finely chop a red onion and a large bunch (about 100g/3½oz) of parsley and toss into the chickpeas. Toast 2 teaspoons of cumin seeds in a dry frying pan (skillet) until fragrant, then roughly crush in a pestle and mortar. Mix 2 tablespoons of sherry vinegar with a good pinch of sugar and plenty of seasoning and the toasted cumin, then mix in 4 tablespoons of extra virgin olive oil. Scatter a bag of wild rocket over the salad, then pour over the dressing and toss to combine.

Roast Peppers with Basil, Cherry Tomatoes & Parmesan

Char 4 red peppers over the flame of a gas hob or under a very hot grill until blackened all over. Pop into a ziplock bag or a bowl covered in cling film and leave for 15 minutes, then peel off the skin and discard along with the seeds. Thickly slice the peppers and arrange on a platter with a large handful of basil leaves, 125g (4½oz) halved cherry tomatoes, some shavings of Parmesan or Pecorino and lots of extra virgin olive oil.

Braised Beans with Extra Virgin Olive Oil

Soak 500g (1lb 1oz) dried cannellini beans in cold water
overnight. Drain and tip into a saucepan, cover with fresh
water and season well. Bring to the boil, then simmer
gently for 1 hour until tender. Drain, but reserve the liquid.
Heat 150ml (5fl oz)extra virgin olive oil in a casserole and
gently fry 2 sprigs of rosemary, 3 crushed garlic cloves,
the pared zest of a lemon and a good pinch of chilli flakes
until fragrant, but not coloured. Tip in the beans and add
enough of the reserved cooking liquid to just cover them.
Simmer for 15 minutes, until slightly breaking down.
Check the seasoning, then serve with grated Parmesan
and a drizzle more extra virgin olive oil.

Whipped Butter Mountain, Sea Salt & Crusty Bread

Allow a pat of unsalted butter to sit at room temperature
for an hour, then beat with a small splash of milk with
a hand-held electric whisk until really light and fluffy.
Beat in some flaky sea salt and serve with a warm crusty
baguette. You can add other flavours if you like, such as
herbs, lemon zest, chilli flakes or garlic, and you can serve
with a drizzle of floral honey.

Dressed Baby Gem Platter

Take 4 baby gem lettuces and cut them into thin wedges.
Arrange on a platter and scatter with toasted pine nuts,
finely grated lemon zest and shavings of Pecorino cheese.
Make a dressing: Whisk the juice of ½ lemon with
1 teaspoon of honey and a crushed garlic clove, then
season well and blend in 4 tablespoons of extra virgin
olive oil. Pour over the platter and serve.

Makes 6 rolls

Prep time: 20 minutes

Tip:

IF YOU CAN GET YOUR HANDS ON A LOBSTER, BY ALL MEANS GO FOR IT, BUT AS WRESTLING WITH A LIVE ONE MIGHT NOT BE PART OF YOUR WEEKEND PLANS, A PACKET OF COOKED PRAWNS WILL DO JUST FINE. A TINY SMIDGE OF FINELY GRATED GARLIC SHOULD SUFFICE IF WILD GARLIC IS OUT OF SEASON.

Prawn & Dill Rolls with Wild Garlic Mayo

You might not think the first choice of companion for a road trip around Ireland would be your dog, but a few years ago, that's exactly who joined me as we filmed a TV show. Escaping the demands of family life with the pup for a couple of days at a time to drive through Ireland's beautiful landscapes was just what the doctor ordered. One of the highlights was an episode shot around West Cork, where I visited food-producing heroes like Sally Barnes of the Woodcock Smokery and Fingal and Gianna Ferguson at Gubbeen Farmhouse. The plan was to shoot one of those picturesque cooking scenes overlooking Kinsale harbour, while demonstrating how to make lobster rolls. It was all going perfectly until the local postman rocked up and Max, who had been diligently posing next to me, did what he does best and chased the poor postie down the road. Chaos, carnage and a lobster roll – what more you could want?

500g (1lb 2oz) cooked cold-water prawns (shrimp)

½ cucumber, peeled, deseeded and finely chopped

2 large sprigs of dill, chopped, plus a few sprigs to serve

1 baby gem lettuce, finely shredded

6 brioche finger buns

Cayenne pepper, for dusting

For the wild garlic mayo

50g (2oz) wild garlic leaves

2 free-range egg yolks

2 tsp white wine vinegar

250ml (1 cup) olive oil

3 tbsp extra virgin olive oil

Lemon juice, to taste

Sea salt and freshly ground black pepper

1. Begin by making the mayo. In a large pestle and mortar, bash the garlic leaves to a paste.

2. In a bowl, whisk the egg yolks and vinegar with some seasoning, then gradually whisk in the olive oil, followed by the extra virgin olive oil, until you have a thick, glossy mayo.

Whisk in 1 tablespoon of just-boiled water, then add the wild garlic paste and season with lemon juice to taste.

3. Put the prawns into a bowl and mix with the cucumber, most of the dill and the baby gem lettuce. Add 4–5 tablespoons of the mayo and toss together.

4. Split the buns and fill with the prawn mixture, then season with a dash of cayenne pepper and finish with a scattering of dill leaves.

Dessert Collection

1. Spiced Rice Pudding with Caramel Oranges
2. Kaiserschmarrn wit h Winter Berry Compote
3. Rhubarb & White Chocolate Croissant Bread Pudding
4. Raspberry & White Chocolate Cheesecake Bars
5. Vanilla Ice Cream & Chocolate Profriteroles
6. Strawberry & Elderflower Victoria Sponge Cake
7. Burnt Basque Cheesecake with Cherries
8. Irish Coffee, Hazelnut & Chocolate Tiramisu
9. Jeni & Craig's Pastry Pie Galette
10. Sprinkles Birthday Cake
11. Ultimate Cookies Three Ways
12. Classic Scones
13. Chocolate Fudge Cake
14. Fancy Meringue Swish
15. Bananas Foster with Vanilla Ice Cream

Serves 4   V GF

Prep time: 15 minutes

Cook time: 1¾ hours

Tip:

THIS MIXTURE ALSO WORKS INCREDIBLY WELL WITH SLOW-BAKED FORCED RHUBARB COOKED WITH VANILLA SEEDS AND ORANGE JUICE INSTEAD OF CARAMELISED ORANGES.

Spiced Rice Pudding with Caramel Oranges

Although I profess to be solely a home cook, I did have a rather brief foray into a professional kitchen when I was 19. I had followed my girlfriend (now wife) Sofie back to her home town of Gothenburg after a whirlwind summer romance, and we both ended up getting jobs on an island fortress called Elfsborg Fästning. One of the jobs I was tasked with was to make a traditional rice pudding called *ris à la malta*, a sweetened rice pudding with orange segments. At the end of the night, Sofie would take her break in the kitchen sitting on a stack of flour bags while I cleaned down the counters. Making this dessert always marked the end of my shift; once the counters were cleaned down, I would get to mixing huge bowls of cooked rice pudding with gently whipped cream, vanilla sugar and cinnamon. This is a slightly fancier version of the classic; I much prefer cooking and sweetening the fruit before stirring through the hot rice.

30g (1oz) unsalted butter

1 cinnamon stick

3 cardamom pods, cracked

175g (6oz) pudding rice

70g (3oz) caster (superfine) sugar

600ml (2 cups) whole milk

Pinch of saffron threads, soaked in 1 tbsp boiling water

Pared zest of 1 orange

75ml (⅓ cup) double (heavy) cream, plus extra to serve

For the caramel oranges

125g (4oz) caster (superfine) sugar

4 blood oranges, peeled and cut into rounds

1. Preheat the oven to 140°C/120°C fan/280°F/Gas 1.

2. Melt the butter in a lidded oven-proof dish over a low heat and gently heat the spices for a few minutes, then add the rice and stir to coat.

3. Add the sugar and milk, along with the saffron and orange zest. Stir and bring to the boil. Cover and bake in the oven for 30 minutes, then remove the lid, stir in the cream and cook for a further 20 minutes.

4. Sprinkle the sugar for the caramel oranges into a separate pan in an

even layer and place over a low heat. Let the sugar melt without stirring, but swirl the pan every so often. Once melted, increase the heat and bubble until you have a rich caramel.

5. Pour in 100ml (scant ½ cup) water (stand back a little, as it may splutter) and stir until smooth. Pour this syrup over the oranges in a bowl and stir to coat, then set aside to macerate and cool.

6. Serve the rice pudding with the caramel oranges and extra cream if you like.

Serves 4   V

Prep time: 25 minutes

Cook time: 15 minutes

A classic winter dessert from the alpine cuisine of Austria, *kaiserschmarrn* is a thick pancake batter that is cooked in a pan before being scattered with boozy kirsch-soaked raisins and then finished in the oven until golden brown. I serve it with a berry compote, which is easily made by simmering frozen fruit with a little sugar and some warming spices. You could add whipped cream or a perfect orb of vanilla ice cream to finish, depending on just how indulgent you feel.

Kaiserschmarrn with Winter Berry Compote

120g (4oz) raisins

75ml (⅓ cup) kirsch (or schnapps)

250g (2 cups) plain (all-purpose) flour

Pinch of salt

6 medium free-range eggs, separated

50g (2oz) caster (superfine) sugar

1 tsp vanilla bean paste

Zest of 1 lemon

350–400ml (1½–1¾ cups) whole milk

50g (2oz) salted butter

Icing (confectioners') sugar, for dusting

For the berry compote

500g (1lb 2oz) frozen berries

60g (2¼oz) caster (superfine) sugar

1 star anise

3 cloves

1. Make the compote first. Put all the ingredients into a saucepan and cook over a low heat for 15–20 minutes until the fruit has started to break down to a lovely thick compote. Spoon into a bowl and set aside.

2. Put the raisins into a small saucepan with the kirsch and heat gently over a low heat, then set aside for at least 15 minutes to allow them to plump up.

3. Sift the flour into a bowl and add a good pinch of salt. Make a well in the centre and add the egg yolks, sugar, vanilla and lemon zest. Start stirring, adding the milk gradually, until you have a smooth batter. It should be thicker than double (heavy) cream.

4. Preheat the oven to 200°C/180°C fan/400°F/Gas 6.

5. In a separate bowl, whisk the egg whites to form soft peaks. Mix a spoonful into the batter to loosen the mixture, then very gently fold the rest into the batter.

6. Melt the butter in a 30cm (12in) non-stick ovenproof frying pan (skillet) over a low heat. Pour in the batter (it will be a very thick pancake) and after a couple of minutes, when you can see it starting to set around the edge, scatter the raisins and booze over the top. Once the underside is set and golden brown and it is cooked about halfway through (you can use a small knife to cut into it to see), pop into the oven for 5 minutes until golden all over.

7. Use a knife and fork to slice the pancake into long, thin shreds, then scoop on to a warmed serving plate. Dust with icing sugar and serve with the compote.

Serves 6–8   V

Prep time: 20 minutes,
plus soaking

Cook time: 50 minutes

Rhubarb & White Chocolate Croissant Bread Pudding

Whenever rhubarb is in season, make sure you grab a bunch of these beautiful pink spears: cook them with sugar and spices before serving with cream-rich rice pud, delicately placing on top of a custard tart or draping atop a stack of French toast. Rhubarb also goes exceedingly well with my croissant bread pudding, made with a rich custard and white chocolate. Make sure you nab yourself some really good croissants; resist the temptation to eat them immediately and you will be rewarded with this showstopper dessert. Try using chocolate croissants instead of plain to give an extra chocolatey hit; you could also add a splash of Baileys or rum to your custard for a grown-up twist.

30g (1oz) unsalted butter, softened

8 fresh all-butter croissants

400ml (1¾ cups) whole milk

400ml (1¾ cups) double (heavy) cream

3 large free-range eggs, plus 2 yolks

40g (1½oz) caster (superfine) sugar

1 tsp vanilla bean paste

120g (4oz) white chocolate chips (or chopped chocolate)

For the rhubarb

500g (1lb 2oz) forced rhubarb, chopped into 3cm (1¼in) chunks

Finely grated zest of 1 orange and juice of ½

100g (3½oz) caster (superfine) sugar

1 vanilla pod, split and seeds scraped

1. Preheat the oven to 180°C/160°C fan/350°F/Gas 4.

2. Put the rhubarb into a roasting tray and scatter over the orange zest and juice, sugar and vanilla seeds. Cover the tray with foil and roast for 20 minutes until tender but still holding its shape. Remove from the oven and allow to cool in its juices to room temperature.

3. Grease the inside of a large (20 x30cm/8 x12in) ovenproof dish with all the butter. Split the croissants in half and stand them, pointy end up, in the buttered dish.

4. Combine the milk and cream in a saucepan over a medium heat and warm until steaming.

5. Put the eggs, egg yolks, caster sugar and vanilla in a large bowl and whisk together, then slowly pour in the hot milk/cream mixture, whisking until fully combined.

6. Pour the hot milky mixture over the croissants and allow to soak for 10–15 minutes.

7. Scatter with the white chocolate and bake for 25–30 minutes until golden and the custard has set but is still gooey. Serve with the roasted rhubarb.

Tip:

IF YOU ARE MAKING THIS AS ONE LARGE CHEESECAKE, TRY SERVING WITH A DELICIOUS RASPBERRY COULIS. PUT 200G (7OZ) MASHED RASPBERRIES INTO A PAN WITH A SPLASH OF COINTREAU OR ORANGE JUICE AND 2 TABLESPOONS OF SUGAR. HEAT UNTIL THE RASPBERRIES ARE ALL BROKEN DOWN, THEN PRESS THROUGH A SIEVE INTO A JUG.

Raspberry & White Chocolate Cheesecake Bars

For a sweet summer pick-me-up, these no-bake cheesecake bars take minimal fuss and are a riff on a recipe I've been making for years, due to the oohs and aahs they almost always garner. You can also make this as one large round cheesecake in a 23cm (9in) loose-bottomed cake tin.

200g (7oz) plain digestive biscuits (graham crackers)

100g (3½oz) unsalted butter, plus extra for greasing

400g (14oz) good-quality white chocolate or chocolate chips

250g (9oz) full-fat cream cheese

200ml (generous ¾ cup) double (heavy) cream

250g (9oz) mascarpone cheese

250g (9oz) raspberries

1. Grease and line a 20cm (8in) square cake tin with baking parchment.

2. Put the biscuits into a resealable bag and bash with a rolling pin until you have fine crumbs. Melt the butter in a large pan, then add the biscuit crumbs and mix to combine. Press the buttery crumbs into the prepared tin and push down firmly with the back of a spoon to create a smooth layer. Chill in the fridge while you prepare the filling.

3. Break 300g (10z) of the chocolate into pieces and put into a heatproof

bowl, in a single layer if you can. Set the bowl over a pan of barely simmering water, making sure the base of the bowl does not touch the water, and gently melt over a low heat without stirring. To check if it is melted, gently nudge a square; if it dissolves, you can stir together. Set aside.

4. Beat the cream cheese, cream and mascarpone in a large bowl with a hand-held electric whisk, then use a spatula to stir the white chocolate through this mixture. Pour over the biscuit base in the tin.

5. Mash half the raspberries to a purée, then push this through a sieve to discard the seeds. Drizzle the raspberry purée over the top of the cheesecake and use a spoon to swirl it into the cream mix. Dot over the remaining whole raspberries, lightly pushing them into the creamy layer.

6. Cover and place in the fridge to chill and set for at least 2–3 hours.

7. Remove the cheesecake from the tin and cut into bars or sqaures. Chop the remaining 100g (3½oz) chocolate and scatter over the bars before serving.

Serves 6–8   V

Prep time: 40 minutes,
plus cooling and
freezing

Cook time: 15–20 minutes

Vanilla Ice Cream & Chocolate Profiteroles

I use this choux pastry recipe for both profiteroles and gougères, and even without a piping bag, you will still get great results. The pastry is worth mastering – it's surprisingly easy once you get the hang of it. Once cooked, the little pastry puffs can be cooled and stored in an airtight container for a day or two, then crisped once more in the oven before filling. I'm a sucker for them filled with crème pâtissière, a rich creamy custard, but as I'm lazy by admission, I often revert to sweetened whipped cream as a less fussy-alternative, or, as here, scoops of vanilla ice cream. Either way, slathered with a rich chocolate ganache topping, I've never had any complaints.

2 x 500g (1lb 2oz) tubs vanilla ice cream

For the choux buns

60g (2¼oz) salted butter

130ml (½ cup) water

80g (3oz) plain (all-purpose) flour

3 large free-range eggs

For the chocolate sauce

60ml (¼ cup) single (light) cream

30g (1oz) caster (superfine) sugar

50g (2oz) dark chocolate (70% cocoa solids), finely chopped

1. Use a spoon or small ice-cream scoop to scoop small balls of ice cream from the tub and place on a tray lined with baking parchment. Freeze the balls until you are ready to assemble.

2. Preheat the oven to 220°C/200°C fan/425°F/Gas 7 and line two large baking sheets with baking parchment.

3. Place the butter in a saucepan over a low heat. Add the water and bring to a steady boil until the butter has melted.

4. Remove the pan from the heat and tip in the flour, beating with a wooden spoon until a dough comes together. Place the pan back over the heat and beat the dough in the saucepan for about 40 seconds. Remove from the heat once again and set aside. Beat one of the eggs in a small bowl.

5. Add the remaining two eggs to the warm dough, one at a time, beating thoroughly after each addition until completely incorporated. Add almost all the beaten egg, a little at a time, until you have a consistency that will hold its shape when piped. It should be smooth, shiny and just about falling from the spoon.

6. Using a spatula, scoop the dough into a large piping bag fitted with a large round piping nozzle. Pipe small dollops of dough (about 2.5cm/1in in diameter) on to the lined baking sheets, leaving about 4cm (1½in) between each one to allow for spreading. Brush each one with the leftover beaten egg.

7. Place in the oven, reducing the heat to 190°C/170°C fan/375°F/Gas 5 for about 15–20 minutes until the choux pastry balls have risen and are golden and crisp.

8. Transfer to a wire rack to cool completely. When cool, use a serrated knife to slice each one in half around the middle.

9. To make the chocolate sauce, put the cream and sugar into a small pan and simmer gently over a low heat until the sugar has dissolved.

Remove from the heat and stir through the chopped chocolate until it has melted and the sauce is silky and smooth.

10. To assemble the profiteroles, arrange the bottom halves on plates or a serving platter, then top each with a small ball of ice cream. Put the lids on, then drizzle with the warm chocolate sauce and serve straight away.

Serves 10   V

Prep time: 20 minutes,
plus cooling

Cook time: 20–25 minutes

Strawberry & Elderflower Victoria Sponge Cake

These days, we are awash with wild, weird and wonderful cake creations, but beyond the modelling chocolate, rainbow fondant and five-tiered feats of engineering, the classics will always be there. One of the first things I learned to bake was a Victoria sponge. A useful trick for getting the ingredient quantities right (and achieving the best sponge) is to remember that the butter, sugar and flour should all be the same weight as your eggs. Weigh your eggs (in their shells) and then weigh out the same amount of the other ingredients. If you find yourself in elderflower season (May and June in the UK), use the floral heads to decorate your cake before serving. This cake is truly the taste of summer.

About 250g (9oz)
unsalted butter, plus extra for greasing

4 large free-range eggs

About 250g (9oz) caster (superfine) sugar

About 250g (2 cups)
self-raising flour

2 tsp vanilla bean paste

½ tsp baking powder

2–3 tbsp natural yoghurt

5 tbsp elderflower cordial

To decorate

250ml (1 cup) double (heavy) cream

4–5 tbsp good-quality strawberry jam

Icing (confectioners') sugar, for dusting

A good handful of fresh strawberries

1. Preheat the oven to 180°C/160°C fan/350°F/Gas 4. Grease two 20cm (8in) deep, loose-bottomed cake tins and line with baking parchment.

2. Weigh the eggs in their shells, then measure out the same weight of butter, caster sugar and self-raising flour. Crack the eggs into a jug and beat together.

3. In the bowl of a stand mixer, beat the butter and sugar with the vanilla bean paste for at least 10 minutes, scraping down the sides occasionally, until really light and fluffy. It shouldn't feel at all grainy when you rub a little bit between your fingers.

4. Gradually beat in the eggs in a slow and steady stream, then fold in the flour, baking powder and yoghurt.

5. Divide the mixture between the two lined tins, flattening the tops with a spatula if needed. Bake in the oven for 20–25 minutes until the tops are nice and golden.

6. Remove from the oven and use a cocktail stick to pierce the cakes all over, then drizzle each one with a tablespoon of elderflower cordial. Leave to cool in the tins for 10 minutes, then turn out on to a wire rack and allow to cool completely.

7. Once the cakes are cold, whip the cream and remaining elderflower cordial together until softly holding its shape. Spread the strawberry jam on top of one of the cakes and top with the whipped elderflower cream. Add the second cake, dust the top with icing sugar and top with some strawberries. This cake will keep well covered in the fridge for 2–3 days.

DESSERT COLLECTION

Serves 10 V

Prep time: 20 minutes, plus cooling

Cook time: 45 minutes

Basque Burnt Cheesecake with Cherries

Many cakes and bakes have 'a moment'; admittedly, I have come a little late to the Basque cheesecake party. However, I arrive fashionably late with the addition of a sweet, zesty cherry compote to cut through the richness of this very simple cheesecake. It's an elegant yet unfussy end to any dinner, and it travels well should you want to impress.

Butter, for greasing

850g (1lb 14oz) full-fat cream cheese

250g (9oz) caster (superfine) sugar

6 large free-range eggs

200ml (generous ¾ cup) double (heavy) cream

2 tsp vanilla bean paste

Pinch of salt

3 tbsp plain (all-purpose) flour

For the cherries

500g (1lb 2oz) fresh or frozen cherries

3 tbsp caster (superfine) sugar

Fincly grated zest of 1 orange and a squeeze of juice

1. Preheat the oven to 220°C/200°C fan/425°F/Gas 7. Butter a 20cm (8in) springform cake tin and line with two sheets of baking parchment crossing the pan so that it is covered completely and the parchment comes up the sides of the tin.

2. Beat the cream cheese and sugar together in the bowl of a stand mixer until silky and no longer grainy when you rub a bit between your fingers.

3. Beat in the eggs one at a time, beating really well between each addition. Scrape down the bowl, then beat in the cream, vanilla and pinch of salt.

4. Sift the flour over the top then mix in, beating for 5 more minutes. Pour into the prepared tin and give the tin a sharp bang on the work surface to release any bubbles. Bake in the middle of the oven for 45 minutes until it is deep brown on top but still has a slight wobble. It will puff up

above the level of the tin, but will fall back after cooking.

5. Remove from the oven and leave to cool completely in the tin; it will fall and crack as it cools.

6. Meanwhile, put the cherries, sugar and orange zest and juice into a small pan and cook over a low heat until you have a thick compote.

7. Cut the cheesecake into slices and serve with the cherry compote. This will keep for 4–5 days in the fridge.

Irish Coffee, Hazelnut & Chocolate Tiramisu

I realise that I've never managed to include my recipe for tiramisu in any of my previous cookbooks. It's one of my go-to desserts to feed a crowd, and has easily earned its place as one of my most-used recipes. Like any recipe that stands the test of time, it's had plenty of variations. I've made this in its most basic form, from a recipe I picked up on my travels in Italy, but I've also served it trifle-style at Christmas, with extra decadent layers of caramel and chocolate custard; sometimes, if I have really good-quality dark chocolate, I'll add a thick layer of shavings as it's assembled. This version is the latest twist and an homage to that favourite after-dinner treat: Irish coffee topped with whipped cream.

400ml (1¾ cups) double (heavy) cream

250g (9oz) mascarpone

4 tbsp caster (superfine) sugar

75ml (⅓ cup) Baileys

300ml (1¼ cups) strong coffee

75ml (⅓ cup) whiskey

200g (7oz) *savoiardi* sponge fingers

100g (3½oz) hazelnuts, toasted and roughly crushed in a pestle and mortar

75g (3oz) dark chocolate, grated

1. Put the cream, mascarpone and sugar into a bowl and whisk by hand with a balloon whisk until it is thick and luscious. Whisk in the Baileys and set aside.

2. Mix the coffee and whiskey together in a shallow dish. Dip the sponge fingers into this mixture and put a layer of them into a glass serving dish. Spread over a third of the mascarpone mixture and scatter with a third of the nuts and chocolate.

3. Repeat to make two more layers, finishing with a layer of cream scattered with nuts and chocolate. Chill for at least 2 hours before serving. This will keep well covered in the fridge for 2–3 days.

Jeni & Craig's Pastry Pie Galette

I have always loved the unique experiences that filming cookery TV shows provides. They are a passport into the kitchens, back-alley restaurants and family homes that you might otherwise never get the opportunity to visit. From the cooking secrets of Italian grandmothers to learning to cook suckling pig in the mountains of northern Vietnam, they have provided formative moments that shape how I cook. One of my favourite filming experiences was closer to home, when I met Jeni Glasgow, her husband Reuven Diaz and their baking muse Craig Thompson. They had recently opened The Brown Hound Bakery, a treasure trove of hand-selected antiques and glass cases carefully filled with chocolate cakes, Boston cream pies and fruit galettes, among other delights. Everything was perfectly curated and truly inspiring. I left with friendship and a pastry recipe that has been present at so many family get-togethers, dinners and celebrations that it deserves a place in this book. I have provided three filling variations for this galette, as it is a wonderfully easy recipe to adapt to whatever fruit is in season.

For the galette pastry

250g (2 cups) plain (all-purpose) flour

25g (1oz) ground almonds

2 tbsp caster sugar

Good pinch of salt

180g (6oz) unsalted butter

1 medium free-range egg yolk, plus 1 medium free-range egg, beaten, to glaze

2 tbsp ice-cold water

1 tbsp demerara sugar, for sprinkling

For the blueberry filling

250g (9oz) blueberries

1 tbsp plain (all-purpose) flour

2 tbsp caster (superfine) sugar

1 sprig of rosemary, needles stripped

Squeeze of lemon juice

For the rhubarb and almond filling

200g (7oz) forced rhubarb, cut into 2.5cm (1in) pieces

100g (3½oz) caster (superfine) sugar

50g (2oz) ground almonds

½ tbsp plain (all-purpose) flour

40g (1½oz) unsalted butter

1 medium free-range egg, beaten

For the vanilla and thyme stone fruit filling

350g (12oz) stone fruit (nectarines, plums, apricots), stoned and cut into wedges

1 sprig of thyme, leaves stripped

1 tsp vanilla extract

2 tbsp caster (superfine) sugar

½ tbsp cornflour (cornstarch)

Pinch of ground ginger

For the Chantilly cream

200ml (generous ¾ cup) double (heavy) cream

1 tbsp icing (confectioners') sugar

1 tbsp brandy (optional)

Continued overleaf

DESSERT COLLECTION

1. For the pastry, place the flour, ground almonds, sugar, salt and butter in a large mixing bowl and, using a pastry blender or a butter knife, cut the butter into the flour until you are left with small pea-sized lumps of butter.

2. In a measuring jug, whisk together the egg yolk, and cold water until combined. Make a well in the centre of the flour and butter mixture and pour in the liquid.

3. Using two large forks, gently toss all the ingredients together until the dough takes shape and begins to hold together. Turn the dough out on to a layer of cling film (plastic wrap) or baking parchment and wrap up. Place in the fridge to chill for a good 30 minutes before rolling out. The pastry dough should still have small visible lumps of butter.

4. **For the blueberry filling**, mix all the ingredients together in a bowl and set aside.

5. **For the rhubarb filling**, toss the rhubarb in 75g (3oz) of the sugar and set aside to macerate for half an hour. In a small food processor, blend together the ground almonds, flour and remaining sugar, then pulse in the butter and half the beaten egg (keep the remaining egg for glazing instead of the whole egg in the pastry recipe). Set aside.

6. **For the stone fruit filling**, toss everything together gently in a bowl and set aside.

7. Preheat the oven to 200°C/180°C fan/400°F/Gas 6. Roll out your pastry between two sheets of baking parchment until you have a large 35cm (14in) round. Remove the top piece of parchment and place the pastry (still on the bottom sheet of parchment) on a baking sheet.

8. Fill the centre with your chosen filling, leaving a 3cm (1¼in) gap around the edge. For the rhubarb, spread with the almond mixture first before topping with the rhubarb.

9. Bring the pastry sides up and over and pinch to seal. Brush with beaten egg and scatter with demerara sugar. Bake for 20–25 minutes until golden brown. Cool for 10–15 minutes.

10. Whip the cream with the sugar and brandy (if using) until it softly holds its shape. Serve slices of the galette with the cream.

The kitchen
is the heart
of the home

Serves 12   V

Prep time: 40 minutes

Cook time: 20–25 minutes

Tip:

MAKE THE SPONGES THE DAY BEFORE AND KEEP IN AN AIRTIGHT CONTAINER OR WRAPPED IN A LAYER OF PARCHMENT AND FOIL. DECORATE ON THE DAY.

Sprinkles Birthday Cake

Birthdays in our house are particularly manic, as our two boys were born days apart, with two years between them, at the end of November and beginning of December. This typically results in a mad week of baking: cupcakes for school and then two birthday cakes to boot. I need a stiff drink after it's all done. To make life easier, I have whittled down my recipes to two basic batters that work a treat and can be transformed with any kiddy paraphernalia needed to cater to the demands and requests of two feral children. The first is this sprinkles batter, a big hit with kids, and despite it fizzing with rainbow colours, it makes a damn good cake and the basis to create whatever wild and weird request your child may demand.

For the sponge

350g (12oz) salted butter, softened

350g (12oz) caster (superfine) sugar

6 large free-range eggs, beaten in a jug

3 tsp vanilla extract

350g (2¾ cups) self-raising flour, sifted

1 tsp baking powder

75g (3oz) rainbow sprinkles (optional)

2–3 tbsp milk or natural yoghurt, to loosen the batter

For the buttercream

400g (14oz) salted butter, softened

½ tsp vanilla extract

600g (1lb 5oz) icing (confectioners') sugar, sifted

To decorate

Lots of sprinkles!

1. Preheat the oven to 180°C/160°C fan/350°F/Gas 4. Grease and line three 20cm (8in) loose-bottomed or springform cake tins.

2. In the bowl of a stand mixer, cream the butter and sugar together until pale and fluffy; it should no longer feel grainy when you rub a little between your fingers. This will take at least 10 minutes – don't skimp on this step, or the cake will not be as light and fluffy as you want.

3. Beat in the eggs a little at a time, beating well after each addition, then add the vanilla extract.

4. Using a spatula, fold in the flour, baking powder and the sprinkles

(if using) until you have a smooth mixture. Use a little bit of the milk or yoghurt if you need to loosen the batter. You want the mixture to be a bit loose and to drop off the spoon with ease.

5. Divide the batter between the three springform tins, flattening the tops with a spatula if needed. Bake in the oven for about 20 minutes until they are golden and springy to the touch. Remove from the oven and leave to cool for a few minutes in the tins before turning out on to a wire rack to cool completely.

6. While the bases are cooling, prepare the buttercream. Beat the butter and vanilla extract together in

a bowl until light and fluffy, then add the icing sugar, a little at a time, until it is all incorporated and the mixture is smooth. Add a little splash of just-boiled water to make it even more luxurious and fluffy.

7. To assemble the cake, place one sponge on a cake stand and top with a layer of the buttercream. Repeat with the other two sponges, then spread a thin layer of the buttercream over the outside of the cake to create a crumb coating. Leave to dry for 10–20 minutes, then spread the remaining buttercream all over the cake.

8. Decorate with more sprinkles and serve.

Tip:

IF YOU WANT TO MAKE THE DOUGH IN ADVANCE, IT KEEPS
BRILLIANTLY IN THE FREEZER, WHERE YOU CAN HAVE IT ON
STANDBY FOR WHENEVER YOU WANT TO BAKE. YOU CAN EVEN
SLICE THE CHILLED DOUGH BEFORE FREEZING: USE A SHARP
KNIFE TO CUT ALMOST ALL THE WAY THROUGH THE DOUGH BUT
STILL KEEP IT IN ONE ROLL AND THEN FREEZE. YOU'LL BE ABLE
TO JUST COOK A FEW AT A TIME.

Ultimate Cookies Three Ways

The beauty of having a really reliable basic recipe is that you can be safe in the knowledge that you can deviate with flavour variations. That's what I've given you here: a great cookie recipe that can be transformed with anything from ground cardamom to orange zest and dark chocolate. I've provided three of my favourites here: dark chocolate and sea salt is the ideal grown-up treat with a strong coffee, while the white chocolate and macadamia is a little sweeter. Now I know cornflake cookies have a whiff of 'internet trend' about them, but I have a deep-rooted love for these chewy yet crunchy biscuits that feel like something a child would dream up. Use the toffees sparingly on top of the cookies (you only really need a small chunk or two to achieve the desired chewiness) and don't forget a sprinkle of sea salt over the top to balance the flavour.

300g (10oz) unsalted butter, softened

150g (5oz) soft dark brown sugar

125g (4oz) soft light brown sugar

225g (8oz) caster (superfine) sugar

2 large free-range eggs

1 tsp vanilla extract

500g (4 cups) plain (all-purpose) flour, plus extra for dusting

2 tsp baking powder

For the dark chocolate and sea salt

100g (3½oz) dark chocolate chips

Pinch of flaky sea salt

For the cornflake toffee

25g (1oz) cornflakes

25g (1oz) chewy toffees, chopped

For the white chocolate and macadamia

80g (3oz) white chocolate chips or chopped white chocolate

25g (1oz) macadamia nuts, chopped

1. Put the butter and sugars into the bowl of a stand mixer and beat together until smooth and light in colour – this will take a good 10 minutes. (If you prefer, you can use a large bowl and a hand-held electric whisk.)

2. Break in the eggs one at a time, beating well after each addition. Once the eggs are mixed in, add the vanilla extract.

3. Sift in the flour and baking powder and mix with a wooden spoon until completely incorporated.

4. Divide the mixture into three, place in three separate bowls and add one of the flavours to each bowl. Use your hands to mix through quickly and bring together into three balls.

5. Roll out each ball on a floured surface into a thick sausage about 20cm (8in) long, then wrap in cling film (plastic wrap), twisting the ends to seal. Each sausage will make 12 medium-large cookies, but you can roll them thinner or thicker to make smaller or larger cookies. Chill the dough in the fridge for 30 minutes before use.

6. Preheat the oven to 180°C/160°C fan/350°F/Gas 4. Line three large baking sheets with baking parchment

7. Slice each dough sausage into 12 discs and place on the trays, making sure there is plenty of space around them as they will spread. Bake for 15–18 minutes, or until they are golden brown at the edges and slightly paler in the centre.

8. Remove from the oven and leave to cool on the trays for 10 minutes, then use a metal spatula to transfer them to a wire rack to cool fully. These will keep for up to 2 weeks in an airtight container.

Food WINS

Makes 16 scones   V

Prep time: 15 minutes

Cook time: 10–12 minutes

Tip:

IF YOU WANT TO MAKE MORE THAN ONE FLAVOUR AT A TIME, THEN DIVIDE YOUR DOUGH INTO TWO AND HALVE THE FLAVOURINGS, OR INTO THREE AND USE ONLY A THIRD OF THE FLAVOURING QUANTITIES.

Classic Scones

Nothing beats a good scone: enjoying them still warm from the oven with butter and jam is one of life's finer pleasures. This recipe works a treat and can be adapted with whatever flavour combinations you fancy – or simply stick to the classic. I often make these for breakfast if we have people staying over. It's the kind of baking that doesn't require too much thinking, and if I'm in a rush, I will simply roll the dough into a round and cut it into triangles, cake-style, to save having to use a cutter.

500g (4 cups) self-raising flour, plus extra for dusting

1 tsp baking powder

Pinch of salt

115g (4oz) salted butter, chilled

3 tbsp caster (superfine) sugar

250–275ml (1–1¼ cups) milk or buttermilk, plus extra for brushing

For the lemon and poppy seed

Finely grated zest of 2 lemons

1½ tbsp poppy seeds

Butter, to serve

For the raisin and orange

125g (4oz) raisins

Finely grated zest of 1 orange

Butter, to serve

For the classic afternoon tea

1 tsp vanilla extract

Clotted cream and strawberry or raspberry jam, to serve

1. Preheat the oven to 220°C/200°C fan/425°F/Gas 7 and line a large baking sheet with baking parchment.

2. Put the flour and baking powder into a bowl with a pinch of salt, then rub in the butter with your fingertips. Add the sugar and the ingredients from your chosen flavouring.

3. Add the milk (you may not need all of it) and bring together with a flat-bladed knife, then use your hands to form a smooth, soft dough.

4. Press out on a lightly floured surface to about 3cm (1¼in) thick and cut out rounds with a 4–5cm (1½–2in) cutter. Reuse the offcuts to make more rounds. Place on the lined baking sheet, brush with milk and bake for 10–14 minutes until risen and lightly golden.

5. Serve warm, with butter or clotted cream and jam.

Serves 12   V

Prep time: 30 minutes

Cook time: 25–30 minutes

Chocolate Fudge Cake

The tradition of making birthday cakes in our house began with my Aunt Erica, who took the creativity reins from my frazzled mother and would allow my brother and I to choose our favourite cake from her dog-eared copy of *Australian Women's Weekly Children's Birthday Cake Book*. They were always memorable; so much so that the tradition continued recently when she made the cake for my brother's wedding. Thankfully, he'd moved on from cakes in the shape of trains decorated with Smarties and colourful popcorn! This is another reliable cake recipe to whip out for special occasions. As it's oil-based, it keeps particularly well and can be made a day or two in advance of decorating. Once you have assembled it, you can take it in any creative direction you wish. Any offcuts from domed tops can be crumbled to make particularly good dirt paths for monster trucks or soil for a garden cake! If you know, you know!

For the chocolate sponge

300g (2½ cups) self-raising flour

40g (1½oz) cocoa powder

1 tsp bicarbonate of soda (baking soda)

230g (8oz) caster (superfine) sugar

5 large free-range eggs, beaten

220ml (scant 1 cup) sunflower oil

225ml (scant 1 cup) semi-skimmed milk

3 tbsp golden (corn) syrup

3 tbsp rainbow sprinkles, to serve

For the chocolate coating and filling

250g (9oz) unsalted butter, softened, plus extra for greasing

175g (6oz) cream cheese

600g (1lb 5oz) icing (confectioners') sugar

45g (1½oz) cocoa powder, sifted

1. Preheat the oven to 180°C/160°C fan/350°F/Gas 4. Grease and line three 20cm (8in) round loose-bottomed or springform cake tins.

2. Sift the flour, cocoa powder and bicarbonate of soda into a bowl. Add the sugar and mix well. Make a well in the centre and add the eggs, oil, milk and golden syrup. Beat well with a whisk until smooth.

3. Pour the mixture evenly into the three prepared tins and bake for 25–30 minutes until risen and firm to the touch. Remove from the oven and leave to cool before turning out on to a wire rack.

4. To make the icing, place the butter in a bowl and beat with the cream cheese until soft and fully combined. Gradually sift and beat in the icing sugar and cocoa powder. The icing should be fluffy and spreadable.

5. Place one sponge on a cake stand and spread a layer of the icing over, almost out to the edges. Repeat with the second and third sponges. Then spread a thin layer of the remaining icing all over the outside of the cake to create a crumb coating. Leave to dry in a cool place (but not in the fridge) for 10–20 minutes, then cover the cake with the rest of the icing.

6. Finish by scattering over the sprinkles. This cake will keep in the fridge for 2–3 days.

Serves 10   V GF

Prep time: 30 minutes, plus cooling

Cook time: 2–2½ hours

Tip:

YOU CAN MAKE THE MERINGUES UP TO 2 DAYS IN ADVANCE AND STORE IN AN AIRTIGHT CONTAINER UNTIL YOU ARE READY TO USE.

Fancy Meringue Swish

My wife Sofie introduced me to this classic Swedish kiddie-style dessert, which I'm guessing is the Scandi version of Eton Mess. It's basically lightly crushed meringues with whipped cream, banana slices and chocolate sauce. My version is slightly more sophisticated, though I don't that say directly to my darling wife. It's a tower of chewy, crisp meringues, piled high with ice cream, whipped cream and warm chocolate sauce. It's wonderfully messy and always garners the best reaction from guests. You can add fresh fruit, flaked almonds or caramelised bananas and passion fruit pulp. Be sure to choose a platter with a generous lip, as this is a messy one to serve – embrace it!

For the meringue

6 large free-range egg whites

325g (11oz) caster (superfine) sugar

1 tsp white wine vinegar

For the chocolate sauce

100g (3½oz) good-quality dark chocolate

30g (1oz) salted butter

50g (2oz) icing (confectioners') sugar, sifted

75ml (⅓ cup) double (heavy) cream

To serve

300ml (1¼ cups) double (heavy) cream

1 tsp vanilla extract

500g (1lb 2oz) tub vanilla ice cream

50g (2oz) hazelnuts, chopped and toasted

1. Preheat the oven to 130°C/110°C fan/260°F/Gas ½. Line two baking sheets with baking parchment.

2. In a stand mixer or using a large bowl with a hand-held electric whisk, beat the egg whites until they form stiff peaks. Gradually whisk in the sugar, a little at a time. Once it is all incorporated, whisk in the vinegar and then continue to whisk on high for 4–5 minutes until you have a smooth, thick, glossy meringue.

3. Dollop large spoonfuls of the mixture all over the baking sheets in sort of giant quenelles (don't worry about being too neat), then bake for

2–2½ hours until you can easily lift a meringue off the paper and they have a very pale shell. Turn off the oven and leave to cool completely inside the oven with the door ajar.

4. When you are ready to serve, make the chocolate sauce. Put the chocolate and butter into a heatproof bowl set over a pan of just simmering water. When melted, remove from the heat and whisk in the icing sugar and cream. Keep warm.

5. Whip the cream and vanilla until it is just holding its shape. Take the vanilla ice cream out of the freezer.

6. Take a large serving platter and dollop a bit of cream on to the bottom and place a meringue on top. Using the cream as glue, pile up the meringues to form a tower. Scoop the ice cream into balls and tuck them into the spaces in the meringue tower.

7. Drizzle the whole thing in chocolate sauce – at the table for extra drama – and scatter with nuts. Serve immediately.

Serves 4   V GF
Prep time: 5 minutes
Cook time: 10 minutes

Bananas Foster with Vanilla Ice Cream

I have a penchant for desserts finished and served at the table, particularly if they are set on fire for added drama. (Although do take care not to lose your eyebrows in the process!) I was lucky enough to first try bananas foster in the restaurant where it was invented, in New Orleans. Brennan's began serving this classic in 1951, and it has endured as one of its most popular menu items. All you need is a tub of ice cream, a bunch of bananas and some hard liquor; the result is sweet, sticky, caramelised bananas that are a simple crowd-pleaser. Cook these à la minute and invite your guests to watch the fun – maybe have a fire blanket at the ready, just in case.

75g (3oz) pecans, roughly chopped

4 bananas, halved lengthways

2 tbsp caster sugar

50g (2oz) demerara sugar

2 tbsp golden syrup

50 g (2 oz) unsalted butter

1 cinnamon stick

1 tsp vanilla extract

50ml (scant ¼ cup) dark rum

Vanilla ice cream, to serve

1. Toast the pecan halves in a dry non-stick frying pan (skillet) over a medium heat, then roughly chop and set aside.

2. Heat a large non-stick frying pan (skillet) over a medium–high heat. Sprinkle the cut sides of the bananas with the caster sugar and place, cut-side down, in the pan. Cook for 3–4 minutes until golden and sticky, then carefully remove to a plate with a palette knife. Add the demerara sugar to the pan in an even layer, along with the syrup. Let them melt together gently, then add the butter and spices and let it all melt to-gether and bubble for 1 minute. Return the bananas to the pan, cut-side down again, and cook for 30 seconds.

3. In a heatproof ladle or small pan, heat the dark rum over a low heat, then light it with a match. Bring both pans to the table and pour the flaming rum over the bananas. Once the flames have died down, serve with scoops of vanilla ice cream and a scattering of pecans.

Index

A

aioli 138–41
  garlic & herb aioli 176
almonds: Jeni & Craig's pastry pie galette 232–5
amatriciana meatballs 168–9
aubergines (eggplants): speedy Parmigiana pasta 61
autumn pasta with blue cheese & nuts 184
avocados: dinner table poke bowl 72–3
  guacamole 66–7
  teriyaki-glazed salmon with rice & greens 74

B

back-to-school slow-cooker chicken stew 30
bacon: amatriciana meatballs 168–9
  Brie, mushroom, truffle & crispy bacon pasta 79
Baileys: Irish coffee, hazelnut & chocolate tiramisu 230
bananas foster with vanilla ice cream 248
banchan: bavette steak with 71
  Korean-cut beef short ribs with 200–1
bang bang poached chicken salad 179
bánh mì Vietnamese turmeric fishcake 65
Basque burnt cheesecake with cherries 229
batter puds 156
beans: braised beans with extra virgin olive oil 205
  kitchen cupboard bean stew 76
beef: amatriciana meatballs 168–9
  bavette steak with banchan 71
  Korean-cut beef short ribs with banchan & rice 200–1
  mustard roast rib of beef 156
  reverse-seared côte de boeuf with aioli & chipped potatoes 138–41
  slow-cooker beef ragu 50
  slow-cooker Mongolian-style beef with sweet potatoes 46
berry compote, winter 216
bitter leaf salad 118–19
blueberries: Jeni & Craig's pastry pie galette 232–5
boulangère potatoes 128
bread: garlic bread 168–9
  garlic toast 50, 87
  whipped butter mountain, sea salt & crusty bread 205

brioche: crispy spice bag chicken buns 203
  prawn & dill rolls 208
  sticky soy pork sliders 130
butter: whipped butter mountain, sea salt & crusty bread 205
butter chicken, slow-cooker 43

C

cabbage: garlicky greens 170–1
  slaw 143–5
cacio e pepe, gnocchi 98
cakes: chocolate fudge cake 244
  sprinkles birthday cake 237
  strawberry & elderflower Victoria sponge cake 224
cauliflower: cauliflower mac 'n' cheese with chorizo crumbs 114
  Sichuan numbing cauliflower wings 198
Chantilly cream 232–5
cheat's hummus salad bowl 191
cheese: autumn pasta with blue cheese & nuts 184
  Brie, mushroom, truffle & crispy bacon pasta 79
  cauliflower mac 'n' cheese 114
  family focaccia-style pizza 134–7
  gnocchi cacio e pepe with mushrooms & sage 98
  green orecchiette with lots of Pecorino 105
  LA kale salad with crunchy Pecorino croutons 62
  Parmesan roasties 170–1
  roast peppers with basil, cherry tomatoes & Parmesan 204
  speedy Parmigiana pasta 61
cheesecake: Basque burnt cheesecake 229
  raspberry & white chocolate cheesecake bars 220
chermoula 160
cherries, Basque burnt cheesecake with 229
chicken: back-to-school slow-cooker chicken stew 30
  bang bang poached chicken salad 179
  chicken & ginger rice soup 33
  chicken satay with sticky rice & steamed pak choi 146
  crispy spice bag chicken buns 203
  French market chicken Sunday lunch 167
  gochujang slow-roast chicken 163
  grilled sticky pomegranate chicken 174
  harissa fried chicken 176
  leftover roast chicken pasta 38

lemony chicken legs with herby yoghurt & crispy crushed potatoes 154
  Noah's chicken noodle soup 36
  oven-roasted shawarma chicken & vegetables 40
  pressure cooker rotisserie chicken pho 88
  rolled chicken breast with stuffing, roasted veg & pan sauce 122–5
  rosemary & thyme confit chicken 118–19
  slow-cooker butter chicken 43
  sticky honey & five-spice slow-cooker chicken 49
  sticky sriracha & ginger popcorn chicken 143–5
chickpeas: cheat's hummus salad bowl 191
  chickpea salad 204
  one-pot Moroccan-style meatballs 53
chicory (endives): bitter leaf salad 118–19
  citrusy harissa barbecued lamb with charred greens 150
chillies: bavette steak with banchan 71
  chilli oil late night noodles 197
  sticky soy pork sliders with chilli & coriander 130
Chinese leaf, clanky herb salad 180
chocolate: chocolate fudge cake 244
  dark chocolate and sea salt cookies 238–9
  fancy meringue swish 246
  Irish coffee, hazelnut & chocolate tiramisu 230
  raspberry & white chocolate cheesecake bars 220
  rhubarb & white chocolate croissant bread pudding 218
  vanilla ice cream & chocolate profiteroles 222–3
  white chocolate and macadamia cookies 238–9
chorizo crumbs, cauliflower mac 'n' cheese with 114
choux buns: vanilla ice cream & chocolate profiteroles 222–3
citrusy harissa barbecued lamb with charred greens 150
clams: one-pan fish & clams with creamy peas & spinach 87
coffee: Irish coffee, hazelnut & chocolate tiramisu 230
compote, winter berry 216
cookies, ultimate 238–9
cornflake toffee cookies 238–9

côte de boeuf, reverse-seared 138–41
courgettes (zucchini): gnocchi al limone
   with courgette, peas & prawns 102
cream: Basque burnt cheesecake with
   cherries 229
   Chantilly cream 232–5
   fancy meringue swish 246
   Irish coffee, hazelnut & chocolate
      tiramisu 230
   rhubarb & white chocolate croissant
      bread pudding 218
   spaghetti with super-creamy mussels 82
   strawberry & elderflower Victoria
      sponge cake 224
   winter sausage meatballs with mustard
      cream, greens & pasta 56
cream cheese: Basque burnt cheesecake
   with cherries 229
   raspberry & white chocolate cheesecake
      bars 220
crispy spice bag chicken buns 203
croissant bread pudding, rhubarb & white
   chocolate 218
cucumber: cucumber platter 204
   pickled cucumbers 200–1
   smacked cucumber 44
curry: chicken satay 146
   slow-cooker butter chicken 43

D
dan dan noodles, Joy on York 108
digestive biscuits (graham crackers):
raspberry & white chocolate cheesecake
   bars 220
dinner table poke bowl 72–3
dumplings: back-to-school slow-cooker
   chicken stew 30

E
eggs: Basque burnt cheesecake with
   cherries 229
   fancy meringue swish 246
   gochujang butter fried rice 91
   instant ramen upgrade 187
   kaiserschmarrn with winter berry
      compote 216
elderflower cordial: strawberry &
   elderflower Victoria sponge cake 224

F
family focaccia-style pizza 134–7
fancy meringue swish 246
fennel: fennel & orange rubbed pork chops
   195

LA kale salad 62
fennel seeds, summer tomato platter with
   toasted 204
fish: caramel salmon feast 68
   one-pan fish & clams with creamy peas
      & spinach 87
   roast brill with brown butter 152
   salmon and tuna poke bowl 72–3
   soy-brined blackened cod with greens &
      rice 192
   teriyaki-glazed salmon with rice &
      greens 74
   Vietnamese turmeric fishcake bánh mì
      65
focaccia-style pizza, family 134–7
French market chicken Sunday lunch 167
fruit, Jeni & Craig's pastry pie galette
   232–5

G
galette, Jeni & Craig's pastry pie 232–5
garlic: garlic & herb aioli 176
   garlic bread 168–9
   garlic mash 96–7
   garlic toast 50, 87
   garlic yoghurt 160
   garlicky greens 170–1
   rosemary & thyme confit chicken with 20
      garlic cloves 118–19
ginger: chicken & ginger rice soup 33
   sticky sriracha & ginger popcorn chicken
      143–5
gnocchi: gnocchi al limone with courgette,
   peas & prawns 102
   gnocchi cacio e pepe with mushrooms &
      sage 98
   gnocchi with soy butter sauce, broccoli &
      sesame 188
gochujang: gochujang butter fried rice 91
   gochujang slow-roast chicken 163
Grannie's lamb shoulder 128
green beans: French market chicken
   Sunday lunch 167
green orecchiette with lots of Pecorino 105
greens: caramel salmon feast 68
   citrusy harissa barbecued lamb with
charred greens 150
   garlicky greens 170–1
   instant ramen upgrade 187
   Joy on York dan dan noodles 108
   pot sticker bowls 112
   soy-brined blackened cod with greens &
      rice 192
   teriyaki-glazed salmon with rice &

greens 74
   winter sausage meatballs with mustard
      cream, greens & pasta 56
guacamole 66–7

H
hasselback potatoes 118–19
hazelnuts: Irish coffee, hazelnut &
   chocolate tiramisu 230
herbs: clanky herb salad 180
   garlic & herb aioli 176
   herby yoghurt 154
hummus salad bowl, cheat's 191

I
ice cream: bananas foster with vanilla ice
   cream 248
   fancy meringue swish 246
   vanilla ice cream & chocolate profiteroles
      222–3
Irish coffee, hazelnut & chocolate tiramisu
   230

J
Jeni & Craig's pastry pie galette 232–5
jok 33
Joy on York dan dan noodles 108

K
kaiserschmarrn with winter berry
   compote 216
kale: green orecchiette 105
   LA kale salad 62
kitchen cupboard bean stew 76
Korean-cut beef short ribs with banchan
   & rice 200–1

L
LA kale salad 62
lamb: citrusy harissa barbecued lamb 150
   Grannie's lamb shoulder 128
   one-pot Moroccan-style meatballs 53
leftover roast chicken pasta 38
lemons: citrusy harissa barbecued lamb
   150
   gnocchi al limone with courgette, peas &
      prawns 102
   lemon and poppy seed scones 243
   lemony chicken legs with herby yoghurt
      & crispy crushed potatoes 154
lettuce: cheat's hummus salad bowl 191
   citrusy harissa barbecued lamb with
      charred greens 150
   dressed baby gem platter 205

fennel & orange rubbed pork chops with browned spring onions & salad leaves 195

little kid/big kid pastina soup 34

M

mac 'n' cheese, cauliflower 114

macadamia: white chocolate and macadamia cookies 238–9

mascarpone cheese: Irish coffee, hazelnut & chocolate tiramisu 230

raspberry & white chocolate cheesecake bars 220

mayonnaise: spicy mayo 72–3

wild garlic mayo 208

meatballs: amatriciana meatballs 168–9

one-pot Moroccan-style meatballs 53

winter sausage meatballs 56

meringue swish, fancy 246

Mongolian-style beef with sweet potatoes, slow-cooker 46

Moroccan-style meatballs, one-pot 53

mushrooms: Brie, mushroom, truffle & crispy bacon pasta 79

gnocchi cacio e pepe with mushrooms & sage 98

mushroom al pastor taco night 66–7

mushroom & tofu rice bowl 111

soy & honey orange mushrooms stir-fry 59

mussels, spaghetti with super-creamy 82

N

nam jim sticky pork with clanky herb salad 180

Noah's chicken noodle soup 36

noodles: chilli oil late night noodles 197

instant ramen upgrade 187

Joy on York dan dan noodles 108

Noah's chicken noodle soup 36

peanut butter pork mince satay noodles 182

pressure cooker rotisserie chicken pho 88

nuoc cham dressing 65

nuts, autumn pasta with blue cheese & 184

O

onions: pork medallions with caramelised onion & mustard sauce 96–7

red onion & coriander salad 174

oranges: citrusy harissa barbecued lamb 150

fennel & orange rubbed pork chops 195

raisin and orange scones 243

soy & honey orange mushrooms stir-fry 59

spiced rice pudding with caramel oranges 214

P

pak choi, chicken satay with sticky rice & steamed 146

pancetta: Brie, mushroom, truffle & crispy bacon pasta 79

slow-cooker beef ragu 50

Parmigiana pasta, speedy 61

pasta: amatriciana meatballs 168–9

autumn pasta with blue cheese & nuts 184

Brie, mushroom, truffle & crispy bacon pasta 79

cauliflower mac 'n' cheese 114

green orecchiette with lots of Pecorino 105

leftover roast chicken pasta 38

little kid/big kid pastina soup 34

Noah's chicken noodle soup 36

prawn pil pil pasta 92

slow-cooker beef ragu 50

spaghetti with super-creamy mussels 82

speedy Parmigiana pasta 61

vodka penne sausage ragu 101

winter sausage meatballs with mustard cream, greens & pasta 56

peanut butter: bang bang poached chicken salad 179

chicken satay 146

Joy on York dan dan noodles 108

peanut butter pork mince satay noodles 182

peas: gnocchi al limone with courgette, peas & prawns 102

kitchen cupboard bean stew 76

leftover roast chicken pasta 38

one-pan fish & clams with creamy peas & spinach 87

peppers: roast peppers with basil, cherry tomatoes & Parmesan 204

pho, pressure cooker rotisserie chicken 88

pickled cucumbers 200–1

pineapple salsa 66–7

pizza, family focaccia-style 134–7

poke bowl, dinner table 72–3

pomegranate molasses: grilled sticky pomegranate chicken 174

popcorn chicken, sticky sriracha & ginger 143–5

pork: fennel & orange rubbed pork chops 195

nam jim sticky pork with clanky herb salad 180

peanut butter pork mince satay noodles 182

pork medallions with caramelised onion & mustard sauce 96–7

slow-roasted pork shoulder with honey & apple vinegar sauce 170–1

sticky pork belly strips supper 44

sticky soy pork sliders with chilli & coriander 130

pot sticker bowls 112

potatoes: boulangère potatoes 128

chipped potatoes 138–41

French market chicken Sunday lunch 167

garlic mash 96–7

hasselback potatoes 118–19

lemony chicken legs with herby yoghurt & crispy crushed potatoes 154

oven-roasted shawarma chicken & vegetables 40

roast brill with brown butter 152

slow-roasted pork shoulder with honey & apple vinegar sauce 170–1

prawns (shrimp): gnocchi al limone with courgette, peas & prawns 102

prawn & dill rolls with wild garlic mayo 208

prawn pil pil pasta 92

profiteroles, vanilla ice cream & chocolate 222–3

prosciutto: rolled chicken breast with stuffing, roasted veg & pan sauce 122–5

pumpkin: autumn pasta with blue cheese & nuts 184

R

radicchio: cheat's hummus salad bowl 191

ragu: slow-cooker beef ragu 50

vodka penne sausage ragu 101

raisin and orange scones 243

ramen: instant ramen upgrade 187

raspberry & white chocolate cheesecake bars 220

rhubarb: Jeni & Craig's pastry pie galette 232–5

rhubarb & white chocolate croissant bread pudding 218

rice: caramel salmon feast 68

chicken & ginger rice soup 33

chicken satay with sticky rice & steamed pak choi 146

dinner table poke bowl 72–3
gochujang butter fried rice 91
Korean-cut beef short ribs with banchan
    & rice 200–1
mushroom & tofu rice bowl 111
soy-brined blackened cod with greens
    & rice 192
spiced rice pudding with caramel
    oranges 214
sticky sriracha & ginger popcorn chicken
    with rice & slaw 143–5
teriyaki-glazed salmon with rice &
    greens 74
rolls, prawn & dill 208
rose harissa: citrusy harissa barbecued
    lamb with charred greens 150
    harissa fried chicken with garlic & herb
    aioli 176
rum: bananas foster with vanilla ice cream
    248

S
salads: bang bang poached chicken salad
    179
    bitter leaf salad 118–19
    cheat's hummus salad bowl 191
    chickpea salad 204
    clanky herb salad 180
    LA kale salad 62
    red onion & coriander salad 174
    slaw 143–5
salsa, pineapple 66–7
satay: chicken satay with sticky rice &
    steamed pak choi 146
    peanut butter pork mince satay noodles
    182
sausages: vodka penne sausage ragu 101
    winter sausage meatballs with mustard
    cream, greens & pasta 56
savoiardi sponge fingers: Irish coffee,
    hazelnut & chocolate tiramisu 230
scones, classic 243
shawarma chicken, oven-roasted 40
Sichuan numbing cauliflower wings 198
slaw 143–5
sliders, sticky soy pork 130
slow-cooker recipes: back-to-school slow-
    cooker chicken stew 30
    slow-cooker beef ragu 50
    slow-cooker butter chicken 43
    slow-cooker Mongolian-style beef with
    sweet potatoes 46
    sticky honey & five-spice slow-cooker
    chicken 49

soups: chicken & ginger rice soup 33
    little kid/big kid pastina soup 34
    Noah's chicken noodle soup 36
    pressure cooker rotisserie chicken pho
    88
speedy Parmigiana pasta 61
spiced rice pudding with caramel oranges
    214
spicy mayo 72–3
spinach: bavette steak with banchan 71
    green orecchiette with lots of Pecorino
    105
    kitchen cupboard bean stew 76
    leftover roast chicken pasta 38
    one-pan fish & clams with creamy peas
    & spinach 87
    vodka penne sausage ragu 101
spring onions: fennel & orange rubbed
    pork chops with browned spring onions
    & salad leaves 195
sprinkles birthday cake 237
squash: autumn pasta with blue cheese
    & nuts 184
    roasted squash platter with garlic
    yoghurt & chermoula 160
sriracha: sticky sriracha & ginger popcorn
    chicken 143–5
stews: back-to-school slow-cooker
    chicken stew 30
    kitchen cupboard bean stew 76
    sticky honey & five-spice slow-cooker
    chicken 49
    sticky pork belly strips supper 44
    sticky soy pork sliders with chilli &
    coriander 130
    sticky sriracha & ginger popcorn chicken
    143–5
    stir-fry, soy & honey orange mushrooms
    59
strawberry & elderflower Victoria sponge
    cake 224
summer tomato platter with toasted fennel
    seeds 204
sweet potatoes: gochujang slow-roast
    chicken 163
    slow-cooker Mongolian-style beef with
    sweet potatoes 46

T
taco night, mushroom al pastor 66–7
Tenderstem broccoli: gnocchi with soy
    butter sauce, broccoli & sesame 188
    gochujang butter fried rice 91
    mushroom & tofu rice bowl 111

pork medallions with caramelised onion
    & mustard sauce 96–7
teriyaki-glazed salmon with rice & greens
    74
tiramisu, Irish coffee, hazelnut & chocolate
    230
toffee: cornflake toffee cookies 238–9
tofu: mushroom & tofu rice bowl 111
tomatoes: amatriciana meatballs 168–9
    family focaccia-style pizza 134–7
    little kid/big kid pastina soup 34
    one-pot Moroccan-style meatballs 53
    prawn pil pil pasta 92
    roast peppers with basil, cherry tomatoes
    & Parmesan 204
    slow-cooker beef ragu 50
    speedy Parmigiana pasta 61
    summer tomato platter 204
    vodka penne sausage ragu 101
tortillas: mushroom al pastor taco night
    66–7

V
vegetables: oven-roasted shawarma
    chicken & vegetables 40
    rolled chicken breast with stuffing,
    roasted veg & pan sauce 122–5
Vietnamese turmeric fishcake bánh mì 65
vodka penne sausage ragu 101

W
whiskey: Irish coffee, hazelnut & chocolate
    tiramisu 230
white wine: one-pan fish & clams with
    creamy peas & spinach 87
    spaghetti with super-creamy mussels 82
wild garlic mayo 208
winter berry compote, kaiserschmarrn
    with 216
winter sausage meatballs with mustard
    cream, greens & pasta 56

Y
yoghurt: garlic yoghurt 160
    harissa fried chicken 176
    herby yoghurt 154
    oven-roasted shawarma chicken &
    vegetables 40
    slow-cooker butter chicken 43

ACKNOWLEDGEMENTS

As with every cookbook, there are a huge amount of unsung
heroes who help bring it to life and of course I would not
have been able to do it without them. Here are the wonderful
folks who have helped bring these recipes to life and this cook
book to fruition:

Firstly, I'd like to give a big shoutout to Olivia, Liz, Vero,
Alice & Sarah at Hodder, and the brilliant team at Hachette Ireland.
Thank you for sticking with me for my 10th cookbook, your
support and encouragement made this project a joy to work on.

I also need to thank Lizzie, my long-suffering food editor &
stylist. You have the patience of a saintwhile helping me to
put shape on the recipe ideas I dream up. Thank you for not only
overseeing the recipes but also styling them and making everything
shine under the camera lens.

To Anne Heffernan and the whole team at Dunnes Stores it has been
a pleasure to work with you as Brand Partner and to have the
support of such an iconic Irish brand. To Daragh Daragh, James
& Emma for keeping everything running so smoothly.

To my favourite Mighty Boosh Gorilla who also takes a decent
photograph and is getting really good at design, Dave Brown,
it was a pleasure to hand over photography duty to you and I
am so thrilled with how you've brought my words to life.
To Clare, for crossing taking the text and patiently correcting
everything and making it just right.

To our brilliant Kate, my fabulous assistant, who saves my
bacon on the daily and keeps the show on the road. You are a
true superhero and of course we couldn't do it all without you.

A special thanks to Vyanne, who makes all our content shine online.
You are the mastermind behind our videos so thank you for
putting shape on all my wild ideas.

To Rosemary & Aoife my agents at United, you have been with
me through thick and thin, and I am so grateful for your
guidance and encouragement.

I also want to thank Nathalie & Julia and everyone at My
This Morning family. Your infectious energy and enthusiasm
every time to cook on the show in London always puts a smile
on my face.

A big thank you to Marc, Robin, Faye, Anne, Dee, Paul & Amy
our brilliant team at Appetite, who make my TV show and so many
others with such passion & pride. Oh, and Barry is your favourite
thing about this book that your name is in it? Thank all for
making me look good(even on the bad hair days and when I insist
on being shot only on my good side).

And last but certainly not least, I want to give the biggest thank
you to my ever-supportive wife Sofie and my beautiful boyos
Noah & Oliver. You are my world and I couldn't do what I do
without your love and support (and all that taste testing!!!).

To everyone who played a part in making this cookbook a reality
and of course you dear reader, I raise a strong negroni to you!
Slainte!

A massive thankyou to Georgia & Luke who cooked through all the
food during our shoot and of course to Polly on props. Also to our
tiny helpers Al, Tiz & Daphne, Bobby & Max for bringing all the
craic to our shoot days. And a special thanks to my mum & Dad &
Sofie's dad Bengt for joining in the fun on the beach and to
John & Katie for coming to film!

First published in Great Britain in 2023 by Yellow Kite
An imprint of Hodder & Stoughton
An Hachette UK company

1

Hardback ISBN 978 1 399 71817 2
eBook ISBN 978 1 399 71818 9

Executive Publisher: Liz Gough
Project Editor: Liv Nightingall
Designer: Dave Brown, apeinc.co.uk
Photography: Dave Brown, davebrown.photo
Food Stylist: Lizzie Kamenetzky
Prop Stylist: Polly Webb-Wilson
Production Controller: Katy Aries

Colour origination by Alta London
Printed and bound in Trento in Italy

Hodder & Stoughton policy is to use papers that are natural, renewable and recyclable products
and made from wood grown in sustainable forests. The logging and manufacturing processes
are expected to conform to the environmental regulations of the country of origin.

Yellow Kite
Hodder & Stoughton Ltd
Carmelite House
50 Victoria Embankment
London
EC4Y 0DZ

www.yellowkitebooks.co.uk
www.hodder.co.uk